the Way *of the* Hen

the Way *of the* Hen
Zen and the Art of
Raising Chickens

Clea Danaan

LYONS PRESS
Guilford, Connecticut
An imprint of Globe Pequot Press

First Lyons Press edition, 2011

Lyons Press is an imprint of Globe Pequot Press

Library of Congress Cataloging-in-Publication Data
is available on file.

ISBN: 978-0-7627-7367-1

This book was conceived, designed, and produced by

Leaping Hare Press
210 High Street
Lewes, East Sussex
BN7 2NS, UK

Creative Director PETER BRIDGEWATER
Publisher JASON HOOK
Art Director WAYNE BLADES
Senior Editor POLITA ANDERSON
Designer BERNARD HIGTON
Illustrator BELEN GOMEZ

Printed in China
Color Origination by Ivy Press Reprographics

10 9 8 7 6 5 4 3 2 1

CONTENTS

INTRODUCTION

I'm sitting in the grass near our baby apple tree. The hard earth beneath my bones supports me. A soft breeze cools my skin. My daughter chatters with animation but tries to sit still. She wants Maisy, our Buff Orpington hen, to come over and peck at a blade of grass grasped in her toddler fist. The chicken eyes her curiously, wary. Finally Maisy struts over and grabs at the long green blade. My daughter grins, her face open and shining. Maisy utters a chickeny question from deep in her throat, then wanders off to join her three flock mates scratching the mulch in search of insects.

A JET ROARS overhead, leaving a streak of white across the wide blue sky. Our neighbor's corgies yip desperately at a passerby or maybe the wind. The Number 10 bus ambles by down the street. Our back garden grows rhubarb, corn, and carrots, has a big compost heap in one corner, and boasts a funky, dark red chicken coop, but we live far from the country.

We live in an ethnically and economically diverse suburban neighborhood on the outskirts of a major metropolitan area. We share a metal fence, carefully covered with bamboo privacy screens, with three sets of neighbors. The houses on our street were built in the 1950s, small "ranch" designs on moderate plots. Not your usual farmland. We moved here to be close to my husband's job at a local hospital. But I, who grew up in more rural settings (though not on a farm by any stretch of the imagination), longed for a more direct relationship with the land and to live a more sustainable lifestyle. So we, like thousands of other urban and suburban residents, decided to raise chickens.

Keeping a small flock of hens seems to be all the rage these

> The most important thing is to express your true nature in the simplest, most adequate way, and to appreciate it in the smallest existence.
>
> FROM *ZEN MIND, BEGINNER'S MIND*, SHUNRYU SUZUKI [1]

days. An Internet search of "chicken keeping" will bring up numerous websites on the subject and Amazon.com sells dozens of raise-chickens-yourself titles to help anyone get started. Trendy magazines wax poetic about the beauty, ease, and general fantastic-ness of brown eggs gathered from your own garden. Much of the fervor comes from a renewed interest in back-to-the-land practices and other ways to live a greener lifestyle. As Susan Orlean writes, "[Raising chickens] was a do-it-yourself hobby at a moment when doing things yourself was newly appreciated as a declaration of self-sufficiency, a celebration of hand-work, a push-back from a numbing and disconnected big-box life." [2] We want a renewed connection with the earth, and greater control over our food. We long for a simpler, more pure life where our souls can

Keeping a small flock of hens seems to be all the rage these days.

> The true purpose [of Zen]
> is to see things as they are, to
> observe things as they are, and
> to let everything go as it goes.
>
> FROM *ZEN MIND, BEGINNER'S MIND*,
> SHUNRYU SUZUKI [3]

breathe freely and our bodies feel in line with the pulse of the land.

One might even say we long for a more Zen existence. In the midst of cell phones that connect to the Internet and cars that tell us where to go, fifty-hour work-weeks and three-hour lines at the airport, we long just to sit on a hill and feed grass to a chicken. Don't you just take a deep breath when you read that? Our true nature is to slow down. Sit. Watch the clouds. Chickens, in their simple scratches and pecks, call us back to our true nature.

Stand in your backyard and hold a smooth, still-warm hen egg in your palm, and you find your body stills. The chatter in your mind becomes quiet. You remember to breathe. In that moment, everything "goes as it goes." The egg, your hand, the chicken fluffing her feathers at your feet.

Whether you are a Buddhist, Christian, Pagan, or following any other spiritual path—or, like me, a combination of various eclectic faiths—your spiritual practice ultimately comes from where you are right now. In Zen Buddhism, this means sitting

*Stand in your backyard and hold a smooth,
still-warm hen egg in your palm...*

> Your life is your practice.
>
> Your spiritual practice does not occur someplace other than
> in your life right now, and your life is nowhere other
> than where you are.
>
> FROM *MOMMA ZEN*, KAREN MAEZEN MILLER [4]

with what is and seeing what it teaches you, where your life leads you right now. For me that means my life as a mother, gardener, writer, and chicken owner is my spiritual practice. My goal, in a spiritual sense, is to bring presence, compassion, and personal growth to all I do.

This book is an invitation for you to do the same. Let what you care about—raising chickens, living a more sustainable life, creating a world where each of us is responsible for our own selves within a larger community—guide your spiritual practice. The stories in this book and the discussions of human nature, spiritual insight, and cultural transformation are all meant to illuminate the spiritual dimensions of the simple practice of raising chickens. Zen Buddhism, because it focuses on presence and compassion, is one of the lenses we will use to look at how raising chickens is a gateway to a more spiritual life. And because I include other facets of spirituality in my own path, a sprinkling of wisdom from other faiths will enter into my discussions. This includes some psychology and studies of human nature, for ultimately all is one.

Raising chickens is not just about raising chickens but is also:

- **A way of taking responsibility for your food choices.**
- **An act of compassion in the face of the way most eggs are "produced" in our industrialized culture.**
- **A declaration of independence—however small—from the food conglomerates that treat animals as commodities.**
- **A political statement in support of a more just and sustainable society.**

ONE CHICKEN AT A TIME

Once you've decided to keep chickens or other small livestock in your own yard, something begins to shift inside you. Not unlike taking up meditation, where the simple act of following your breath releases you into new layers of self, raising chickens begins to reveal the assumptions we carry in our culture about life, death, food, and personal responsibility.

THIS BOOK EXPLORES some of those discoveries. What does it mean to take responsibility? Why are so many people called to this simple task of being an urban chicken farmer right now? And what can our feathered friends, and the art of caring for them, teach us about ourselves? Whether you have been raising chickens for years or are just considering the

From the moment the sun comes up, we are in constant
search of enlightenment. Picking, scratching, digging, and
pecking are all studied exercises of this long-standing tradition
of exploration as well as the source for nourishment.
By becoming more mindful of the source of our nourishment
and enjoying the pathway of gathering, we grow the spirit.

FROM *YOGA FOR CHICKENS*, LYNN BRUNELLE [5]

possibility, this book will help you look more deeply at how
you can make your life your spiritual path. Even the simple
task of caring for a flock of hens can widen your perspective.

Chickens never try to do or be anything than who and
what they are. They never step out of their chicken-ness,
and as such all they can do is fully express their true nature.
But their very chicken-ness keeps them from "being Zen,"
for because they are so fully chickens, they cannot witness
their chicken-ness. So chickens themselves are in some ways
quite Zen, and in most ways not Zen at all (how Zen is that?).
But because chickens represent something, a certain way
of life, a new choice for living on a small planet, we can turn
to raising them as a sort of guide toward a more spiritual life.

So, come and join me on the grassy hill by the apple tree,
and let us see what a little flock of hens can teach us. Let us
see how we might change the world and ourselves, one step,
or rather one chicken, at a time.

CHAPTER ONE

THE SOUND OF ONE WING FLAPPING

What is the sound of one hand clapping?
This classic Zen koan brings us into the possibilities
of the deepest silence, the space beyond silence, to unity
with the Great Mystery. The sound of one wing flapping,
however, is not silent at all—as you will know if you have
ever tried to capture a reluctant chicken. Flap, flap, flap.
The chicken announces her presence with sleek, feathered
determination. The chicken is here! What possibilities
abound? What can she teach us about new ways of living
in harmony with each other, the earth, and ourselves?

WINGS OF CHANGE

◆

We live in an exciting time, in which our actions truly affect the health and well-being of the entire rest of the globe. How you or I choose to live each day—each big or small choice about how we eat, travel, stay warm, educate our children, clean our homes, and so on—creates one world or another. Through our individual and collective decisions, we can create a world that will sustain us and provide for us in the long term, or one that will perish.

AT TIMES it is difficult to discern which of our choices is the more environmentally conscious or compassionate or politically correct or best for our health. Often it even seems that our actions create conflicts among those goals, as when choosing whether to be vegetarian or to use cloth diapers or deciding which vehicle to drive. In a global world, our choices, our decisions, and the consequences that follow can thoroughly overwhelm us as individuals.

But finally there's a choice that makes sense on all counts. That one flapping wing, though its lift is minimal, suggests a flock of positive consequences, including compassionate, healthy living, and ecological benefit. That little wing stirs up a dust storm of change as we welcome the possibilities of chickens as pets, food producers, and backyard allies. What is the sound of one wing flapping? The sound of right relationship and conscious living on the planet.

Ancient Chicken Koans

ko'an (ko'-an) n. (Jap.) a paradoxical question
The word koan literally means "a public document."
This actually has roots in chicken-ness. Our public
display of practicing mindfulness has been on view
in farms, coops, and backyards for millions of years,
but only recently has any attention been drawn to
our depth. Now, a koan has come to mean a form of
pondering based on the actions of famous poultric
masters. It is a baffling riddle with no answer,
no logic, and no connection.
Ponder these imponderables:
Why did the chicken cross the road?
What is the sound of one wing flapping?
Which came first—the chicken or the egg?
Is an empty nest really empty?

FROM *YOGA FOR CHICKENS*, LYNN BRUNELLE [6]

The sound of one hand clapping invites us into the silent
void of non-dual consciousness, or unity with God. But while
this may be the ultimate goal of our spiritual journey, right
here and now on this planet we live in a relative world. This
means we live in bodies, in a community, and we eat food
made on the planet. We must hold both worlds, relative and
absolute, when looking at the bigger picture of what it means

to do anything, including raising chickens. Our connection with Spirit comes through our daily lives and through healthy unity with others as well as the vast Silence. The sound of one hand clapping is a path to enlightenment; the sound of one wing flapping is a path to a conscientious and enlightened world.

So, on a relative level, let us examine why we should raise chickens to foster a new world of compassion and integration. First, what are the reasons that people choose to raise chickens?

WHY RAISE CHICKENS?

People choose to keep chickens for a plethora of reasons. Keeping a small flock has become an easy and fun way to meet a variety of dreams. Most chicken owners want to live a life in tune with the land, their food, and the cycles of life. Some want their children to grow up knowing where their food comes from, or to develop the responsibility that comes from caring for a pet. For others keeping a flock of hens reminds them of childhood visits to their grandmother. For most it is a promise to slow down long enough to gather eggs. To watch a chicken scratch the soil. To laugh more, give thanks more, love more.

CHICKENS are multipurpose animals. They are easy to keep, provide us with manure and eggs, don't take up much space, and they are fun to watch. Raising them teaches us about life and death. It allows us to participate more actively in our own food cycle—but we don't have to slaughter another being to do so. Chickens offer us a middle ground: because a small flock can be kept in a small yard, we don't have to move to a farm to conduct a more conscious life in greater attunement with the natural world. We get our own little farm right here on our urban plot.

For most people, though, the joy of keeping chickens is still a well-kept secret. The announcement that you plan on ordering chicks in the spring is met with excitement among sub-cultures of animal lovers, organic gardeners, and urban farmers, but for most mainstream people, it may still seem a little bit odd. We have so compartmentalized our lives, putting food over here, hobbies in this corner, and pets inside our well-heated homes, that the ability to combine them all

Chickens do not always enjoy an honorable position among city-bred people, although the egg, I notice, goes on and on. Right now the hen is in favor. The war has deified her and she is the darling of the home front, feted at conference tables, praised in every smoking car, her girlish ways and curious habits the topic of many an excited husbandryman to whom yesterday she was a stranger without honor or allure.

FROM "THE HEN: AN APPRECIATION," E.B. WHITE [7]

in one fell swoop boggles the mind. Before the 1950s, keeping chickens in one's urban or suburban backyard was not uncommon, though as E.B. White attests, raising hens goes in and out of style. After World War II, as science took center stage, from television to Sputnik to antibiotics, the earthy hen lost favor. Today we again find her pecking and scratching in the trendiest of urban yards across the globe.

Eggs from Our Own Garden

When I was a girl, my best friend had chickens in her backyard. I loved to take a little basket out to the coop to look for eggs. It scared me a little if there was a hen inside the nest box. I wasn't brave enough to reach underneath their soft bodies. Nor was I brave enough to step inside the run. But tossing treats inside and watching the birds scramble and scratch was great fun.

YEARS LATER I studied organic gardening and volunteered at an organic farm. One afternoon the task fell to me to feed some weeds to the new flock of chicks. Stepping into the warm, barnyard-smelling shed and being charged by two dozen five-week-old chicks made my heart race. Real chickens! I didn't know it yet, but I was in love. I had caught chicken fever, although it took some time for the symptoms to show up. The idea of keeping hens myself formed slowly. I wanted the cozy feeling of a farm life—without the enormous cost and responsibility of a farm. I wanted my children to grow up knowing not only where a tomato comes from, but also about eggs and other sources of protein. I still remembered my childhood friend's flock, and I wanted my children (and me!) to know the pride and fun of gathering eggs from our own yard. We had little money, though, and I wasn't sure how we could afford a manufactured coop costing three hundred dollars or more. I learned about a smooth-looking plastic coop that comes in an array of snappy colors, but decided I wanted more than the two hens it accommodated. My aim was for a more bucolic-looking coop. I wanted to build it myself, but balked at my rudimentary carpentry skills and, although my husband gave me an electric saw for my birthday to encourage me, we were not sure where the wood would come from.

Then a friend of mine offered for free a heap of scrap wood that she had inherited with her house. Our husbands hauled it over to our backyard, where it sat for a month or two, christened in several spring snows. I stared at the hodgepodge of boards, piling them and unpiling them, coming up with a design for our little hen house. I was determined to make our own coop, however Robinson Crusoe it might end up looking. The little house began to take shape in my mind. I researched chicken breeds that were mellow in disposition, good layers, and cold-hardy. I chose four breeds—Buff Orpington, Black

Austrolorpe, Rhode Island Red, and an Easter Egger—and ordered a shipment of chicks with a friend to save on shipping costs. I made arrangements to borrow a dog crate from another friend in which to rear the chicks.

Once they were safely installed, I did the math—my chicks would have all their true feathers and be ready to go outside in mid-May. I had until then to craft a little predator-proof home out of my heap of wood and old shelves. Meanwhile our four chirping fluff balls serenaded my writing time from their dog crate on the office floor. We kept the cats out of the room and taught our daughter to hold the chicks gently.

Finally we could put it off no longer. While our then three-year-old played in the yard (I gave her a packet of carrot seeds to keep her occupied, and we had carrots popping up in all sorts of strange places that spring), my husband and I patched together a funny little coop with an egg door and a roost. It was the first building project we had accomplished together, and afterward I boasted that "two Aquarians can build a chicken coop without killing each other." I felt such a swelling of pride at our resourcefulness.

Resources & Resourcefulness

Keeping chickens, I was to discover, is all about being resourceful, or full of resources. When I decided to try my own hand at chicken husbandry, I did it to have the resource of fresh, more nutritious eggs from my own backyard. In the process, however, I learned about the many resources I could already draw on: my friends, with their wood and experience and a dog crate; my marriage, that could last the efforts of building a coop; an excellent local feed supplier; a local online urban-farmer group that could help me fight for the legalization of chickens; and even my own reserves of energy, which proved enough to chase a child and craft a coop while being six months pregnant.

Resource means to go back to the source again. Having chickens in the backyard is about returning to a time when we held responsibility for our own resources. It's about the ability to produce food in your own yard. It's about being able to walk out the backdoor on a cool spring morning, flip open the hinged nest-box door and find a smooth, brown egg for breakfast. On the perfect day, I cook these dark-yolked eggs with a fresh tomato and some herbs picked also in my own garden. I have lost my childish fear of hens, but their girlish ways and sweet brown eggs delight me in just the same way as they did when I first started raising chickens.

I'm proud to do something just a little bit different from the usual ideas of what a woman can do in her suburban yard and be a part of the wave of change that says we can create a world of sustainable resourcefulness and renewed responsibility.

Keeping chickens, I was to discover, is all about being resourceful, or full of resources.

OVERTURNING THE REALM OF ILLUSION

◆

Why at this time are we collectively turning to chickens in our quest to "break down the cave of ignorance?" Into the no sound of one wing flapping steps a possibility for a new life, for the breakdown of duality that has separated farmers from everyone else. We open to new possibilities and free ourselves from the basket we have woven out of industry and automation. Why?

WHENEVER I QUESTION WHY a person or a group makes certain choices, I find much of the answer in the study of Spiral Dynamics, a system of looking at human nature created by American psychologists Drs. Clare Graves and Don Beck. Clare Graves said, "[The] psychology of the mature human being is an unfolding, emergent, oscillating, spiraling process, marked by progressive subordination of older lower-order behavior systems to newer higher-order systems as man's [*sic*] existential problems change."[8] Don Beck took the complex system of categories Graves created and applied a more accessible system of phases of development—called memes—to examine why and how a person, community, or institution relates to a particular issue or circumstance. While it is not my purpose to go into the entire system of memes or memetics here, I find it useful to apply Spiral Dynamics to our question of why raising chickens has suddenly become so popular. It helps us to see the deeper layers of a simple trend.

What Is the Sound of the Single Hand?

When you clap both hands together, a sharp sound is heard; when you raise the one hand, there is neither sound nor smell. Is this the High Heaven of which Confucius speaks? Or is it the essentials of what Yamamba describes in these words: "The echo of the completely empty valley bears tidings heard from the soundless sound?" This is something that can by no means be heard with the ear. If conceptions and discriminations are not mixed within it, and it is quite apart from seeing, hearing, perceiving, and knowing, and if, while walking, standing, sitting, and reclining, you proceed straightforwardly without interruption in the study of this koan, you will suddenly pluck out the karmic root of birth and death and break down the cave of ignorance. Thus you will attain to a peace in which the phoenix has left the golden net and the crane has been set free of the basket. At this time the basis of mind, consciousness, and emotion is suddenly shattered; the realm of illusion with its endless sinking in the cycle of birth and death is overturned.

FROM *THE ZEN MASTER HAKUIN*, YABUKOJI [9]

23

The recent resurgence of small-scale chicken ownership speaks to a larger movement toward increased responsibility for ourselves, our communities, and the land. Again, it's a question of resources, the what and the how. Before the 1950s, keeping chickens in one's yard was a reflection of the culture's attention toward family units and survival. Then our focus turned outward: into the realms of business, a global economy, and even the control of space beyond the planet. These pursuits taught us much as a species about what it means to be alive—and what our responsibilities are as human beings. Today our culture is evolving toward goals of mutual growth, interdependence, and the survival of the earth. We see that we must be more aware of each other and of the planet. We must work together to move beyond warfare, conquest, and domination over others, or we will wipe out our species (and probably a whole lot of other species in the process).

I know what you are thinking. Um … they're just chickens. But now think a bit more about what raising chickens in one's backyard actually accomplishes:

- **Growing some of one's own food instills a sense of responsibility for oneself, for the food source, and for the resources needed to grow that food.**
- **Keeping animals that are both pets and a food source develops compassion and gratitude.**

• **When you know where your food comes from and you know what goes into that food, you know your body better, and are more likely to make healthful choices.**
• **Free-range chickens teach us about cycles of food, life, death, and nature.**

In short, we see clearly how we are interconnected with the food that we eat, and the planet. Our actions affect our health, the health of those around us, and the health of the earth. At this phase of evolution, we are overturning the illusion that we are separate beings who can do whatever we want. Raising chickens is a vote for a more compassionate, nature-based economy. It is an education in interconnection, responsibility, and compassion. Living in relationship with chickens illustrates clearly how we are separate yet together, interdependent beings—what Suzuki-roshi called "a complete flashing into the vast phenomenal world" [10]—who fold into each other within the vastness.

Chicken Enters the Gate

One day, as Chicken stood outside the gate, the farmer called to her, "Chicken, chicken, why do you not enter?"

Chicken replied, "I do not see myself as outside.

Why enter?"

FROM *YOGA FOR CHICKENS,* LYNN BRUNELLE [11]

Digging Deeper

◆

Organic gardening has become the buzzword of the growing world. Everyone from President Obama to Prince Charles, not to mention the little old lady down the street and your children's school, is eschewing chemicals and turning to methods more in tune with the natural order of how things grow. We want to grow healthier food and have a greener earth. We want our children to grow up healthier, too; organic foods reduce the risk of all manner of illness from the common cold to cancers. Since a big part of the organic garden is natural fertilizer, it's only natural that the next step in the garden and backyard includes your own little flock of fertilizer producers.

W HEN MY PULLETS grew out their big-girl feathers, they graduated from the dog crate in the office to their newly finished coop—and my backyard graduated from homestead into a hobby farm. Though we supplement with bagged feed from a local feed supplier,* by bringing chickens into the yard we created a whole system that could in theory run by itself. The chickens fertilize the yard. They run around, scratching at the mulch, the compost, and the garden beds in search of greens

---

* It took me a while to find our local feed store because it's been around so long and is so not modernized that it didn't come up on Google Maps, doesn't have a website, and doesn't use a computer system. The man who runs it is past eighty. He doesn't take credit cards. He fixes up old lawnmowers to stay in business, but I imagine in the store's heyday it was the center of farm life. You can still buy meat birds and roosters from him, though he's surrounded by a housing development and shopping malls. His existence makes me happy—and not just because he sells chicken feed on my side of town.

> The combined average percentages (per total weight)
> of aged chicken manure and litter … is about 1.8 nitrogen,
> 1.5 phosphate, and 0.8 for potash.
>
> WWW.POULTRYONE.COM [12]

and insects. I toss kitchen scraps into the coop or the compost and they turn it into food for the microorganisms that feed the plants that will eventually find their way onto my dinner table.

On an ecological level, raising chickens is a whole system; we actively participate in the cycle of life, egg to table, chick to hen, with nothing wasted. But viewed through the lens of quantum physics or transcendental consciousness, the whole system is even more. We, in our human mind, see the chicken as a chicken. The manure is manure, containing set percentages of nutrients to put in the garden, which is a garden. But seen on a vaster time frame, the chicken is a chicken for only a blink of time. Her egg "exists" for an even shorter blip before it becomes a part of me. Her droppings rather quickly become what we call the gardens and backyard. The soil becomes the plant. The plant becomes part of me, and of the chicken. Then of the compost. On and on it flows, a whole system dancing through time and space.

If our species can begin to step free of the boundaries we tend to live within, and see each garden, our individual lives, the planet, even the entire universe as a whole intertwined system, then we can begin to live sustainably. Sustainability is another buzzword, one that means our actions and choices will lead to a life that can continue to cycle and beget new cycles. Sustainability is about renewable resources, zero emissions, zero population growth, and the elimination of waste.

To live a sustainable life, we must be able to see beyond ourselves and make choices that benefit others as well— a central part of the spiritual notion of compassion. "For interdependence is the first law of compassion, which is in turn the fullest expression of the spiritual life of human beings," writes theologian Matthew Fox.[13] Raising chickens is a sustainable (compassionate) behavior because:

- **A small backyard flock is a whole system.**

- **Keeping a small flock in a suburban or urban setting is manageable by one person or family.**

- **It produces small amounts of waste that are not waste (as opposed to the huge quantities of non-manageable and therefore polluting chicken poo produced by factory farms).**

- **It has a very small carbon footprint, depending on how much you supplement your flock with outside food sources.**

We must be careful, though, for sustainable does not mean "closed system" any more than compassion does. Picture your circulatory system. When all is well, the blood stays inside your arteries and veins, pumping around and around, through and by the heart. But this system requires some input from outside itself—water, nutrients, and oxygen, to name a few—and its health also depends on the expulsion of unneeded materials, which are cleansed by the kidneys.

So like a circulatory system, a little chicken hobby farm is a system unto itself that is also part of a larger system. Writes green economist Herman E. Daly, "Sustainability is a way of asserting the value of longevity and intergenerational justice, while recognizing mortality and finitude." [14] I, the chicken farmer, am finite, but my actions occur within the flow of many generations. I am a part of a larger whole, and thus must not only value my own mortality, but the intergenerational justice of living compassionately on the earth. Living sustainably, as Daly defines it, is also living compassionately.

This is why organic gardening and urban hobby farming have become so "trendy" of late. They are practices that marry survival with sustainable and compassionate living. They are choices that represent our spiritual urge to live in right relationship while also meeting our practical needs. In doing so, they bring us more deeply into a spiritual life.

Also popular today is the local food movement, a call to reduce our carbon footprint by eating locally grown food. Local can be defined in a number of ways, from the backyard or a nearby community garden, to grown and processed within

fewer than 50, 100, or 250 miles (80, 160 or 400 km). In the U.S., food often travels hundreds, even thousands, of miles— from as far away as Kenya. The distance the food travels from farm to table is referred to as food miles. Reducing that distance reduces one's carbon footprint and keeps money local. Local food not only reduces our ecological impact; it means more nutrient-rich food that has not been sitting around, been shipped, or been frozen. It tends to mean getting your food from smaller farms that lean toward organic practices or are organic-certified. It exemplifies the sustainable compassionate system, the circles of interconnection that our food and our other needs depend on.

Obviously a backyard and chicken coop qualify as local. "I think this intense interest in keeping chickens for their wonderful eggs, and compost-making abilities, as well as their uniqueness as pets with considerable personality, has surfaced with the concern about our corporately controlled food supply," writes Carol Ann Sayle in the *Atlantic*.[15] As a culture (or at least a chicken enthusiast sub-culture) we have tired of letting someone else select our food and where it comes from.

Variety is another benefit of local food. A visit to your farmers' market might reveal several varieties of heirloom tomatoes, "California Wonder" bell pepper plants, or hand-picked, wild morel mushrooms from nearby forests. The bright colors and choice of varieties are not limited to plants, however; small-flock chicken farmers offer a rainbow of beautiful eggs one cannot buy at the supermarket.

More local even than a farmers' market, however, is your own backyard. My daughter brought me a just-gathered egg one afternoon. "A fresh chicken egg," she said, her lips a thin line of satisfaction. I thanked her and put the egg in the refrigerator. I thought, "not truly fresh, not as fresh as they get"—for the egg was cold. That is when I knew I'd become spoiled. A truly fresh and local egg (despite what the boxes at the market proclaim) is one that is still warm, maybe even still damp from the hen. A hen I can stroke and thank and toss a treat.

A CHICKEN PERSON

It is said there are cat people and there are dog people. To these I add another category: the chicken person. A chicken person names her birds. She talks to them, coos to them, strokes them. She delights in the softness of their feathers and lovingly strokes their surprisingly warm, scaly legs. A chicken person knows that a hen's eyes are really rather beautiful. She learns the different clucks and their meanings, and when she gathers eggs she tosses in a few treats and thanks her birds for their contribution.

THE PET ASPECT of the urban chicken is another reason for their increasing popularity. Chickens have personalities. They stare you in the eye and ask boldly for treats. They talk back. They follow you around the yard and take feed from your hand. Taking care to avoid their strong claws, my daughter and I both love to hold our chickens. She and her friends can spend an hour or more chasing the birds around the yard, catching them, stroking them, and letting them go. Our son, an infant as I write this, stares at them with drool-lipped fascination and says, "Euhhhhh."

Even our rather spoiled cats have had to welcome our birds into the family. One of our birds seems to suffer from less-than-optimum chicken intelligence (no, they are not smart, but they are not as stupid as everyone thinks), and she loves to follow our male cat around the yard. They are almost the same color, a mottled gray, though she has orange in her feathers, too. Gryphon complains with an irritated meow, his ears flattened slightly in resignation rather than hostility, as Millie trots along behind him as if cajoling him to play. Our hens are fully part of our family, albeit members who live outside the main house.

And yes, we do keep our hens strictly outdoors, though when the door is left open, they sneak in when we're not looking. We shoo them out to avoid chicken droppings in the kitchen. Some chicken owners don't draw such a line. On MyPetChicken.com, for twenty-five dollars you can purchase a custom-sewn chicken diaper in six bright colors and five sizes. Says the site, chicken diapers are, "Great For: Injured hens that need to recuperate indoors; show birds that need to be separated from the flock in the months before the show;

[and] beloved family pets who you couldn't dream of putting outside."[16]

There is something magical about a hen house in a suburban or urban setting.

I've often complained that our cats don't pull their weight. I imagine them standing on a chair at the kitchen sink, long, skinny rubber gloves pulled up to their armpits, washing up the dishes. It would begin to cover the cost of their outrageously expensive food. Chickens don't quite pay for themselves, not a small flock anyway, but they do offer both the benefits of pets and of a farm animal.

In a world that demands multipurpose everything, such as the camera-phone that plays the music of a thousand CDs, chickens suits us. They lay eggs. They fertilize. They amuse. They're far more cuddly than a fish or a turtle. Most importantly, they provide a melding of lifestyles, country meets city or suburban plot. No longer must you be either a country or a city mouse; thanks to the chicken, you can be both. The chicken is leading us to blur the lines we've drawn between different lifestyles and socioeconomic classes.

The Urban Hen House

There is something magical about a hen house in a suburban or urban setting. The unexpected juxtaposition is like a boat in the desert. Besides shocking us out of complacency, it refreshes. We consider that a life a little off-center is possible, even desirable.

Urban Chicken Sites:

www.urban-chickens.com

www.urbanchickens.net

www.backyardchickens.com

www.thecitychicken.com

www.mypetchicken.com

www.organic-gardening-and-homesteading.com

My friends think that if I brought the farm into my backyard, so too might they. If it's possible to marry the country and the city, what else might be possible? Urban chickens offer the best of both worlds, and they lead us to consider what other creative possibilities await us.

When people visit us, they gaze out the sliding glass doors off our tiny dining room, and they say, "Oh, your chickens!" They ask all sorts of questions, and smile with delight as we discuss how easy our birds are to care for. They comment on how pretty the birds are, not at all what they thought. They admire our little dark red coop, and they ask if the neighbors seem bothered by the noise. I assure them that our neighbors seem to appreciate our chickens (we don't have a rooster), who are rarely noisy. We discuss the yard and the eggs, and share stories about beloved hens from the past or how much our visitors dream of having a little flock of their own, too.

Urban chickens connect people. They provide something to talk about and doorways into new ways of living. They fit our lifestyles so well. Underneath the fast-paced, high-tech world is a desire to connect. The urban chicken provides this.

Many of today's technologies focus on connecting to the global network without leaving home. At this time in history, we are both more a part of the world and more home-centered because of these technologies: we can talk to a person on the other side of the world through video-conferencing, then play ball with our child in the backyard with barely a break in between. On a spiritual level, this interconnection leads to some interesting implications: we are all one, yet occupy our own space. We also begin to understand how our choices regarding basic survival such as food and health operate at home but within a larger, interdependent world.

In struts the chicken. The move toward raising your own small flock of chickens demonstrates the shift our culture undergoes as we examine the implications of living on a planet with more than six billion other people and still growing. Goals of mutual growth, interdependence, and the survival of the earth have become foremost in our minds, while our hearts yearn to stay at home and live the simple life. Keeping your own hens (and, for some, the occasional rooster) meets both of these goals. Brought into the city in the age of the Internet, the urban chicken heralds a wholly new era of high-tech meets back-to-the-land.

What is the sound of one wing flapping? It is the sound of a dust storm of change that overtakes your existence. It is a life of having your seed cake and eating it, too. It is the call to live feather-light on a growing, living planet.

CHAPTER TWO

CHICKEN MIND, BEGINNER'S MIND

Beginner's mind is the Zen concept of approaching something without preconceived notions, labels, or ideas. One's mind is open as a beginner's. Chickens have a way of inspiring beginner's mind. As I watch my hens strut around the yard, scratching for insects and gobbling down grass, I enter a place of delighted calm. Their simple needs become my simplified needs. I take a deep breath and settle into the moment. I am content just to sit. As we've seen, our relationship with the chicken is a complex one; and yet it is a calming and simple relationship that takes us back to ourselves.

MEMBERS OF THE FAMILY

◆

By bringing chickens into our urban and suburban families, we are saying something about our relationship with nature, the human world, and our spirits. We want our homes to represent our relationships with ourselves and others. That relationship can then also be a source of healing and spiritual well-being. When we "walk our talk" (about health, ecological responsibility, and so on) we become more whole ourselves.

ZEN TEACHER and author Charlotte Joko Beck writes, "any intimate relationship, if we view it as practice, is the clearest mirror we can find." [17] Pet chickens provide a certain intimacy that can be afforded only by something that is both pet and food source, a rare combination. They become a mirror, then, showing us our true nature. They teach us about responsibility on a deep level. They need us and we need them. They are easy to care for, yet offer great rewards for our efforts. People who care for chickens may not realize that they are living compassionate lives in touch with the earth, but hen-keeping has become part of their spiritual practice.

If your life is your practice, then anything can be approached as spiritual. The way you approach something simple and everyday, like your chickens, is how you approach everything else. Since your hens are a fairly low-stress part of your life, a place of joy and connectedness, they can be a gentle way to observe your own mind and offer you clues to how you deal with the rest of life. They become a mirror in which to see your relationship with yourself and other areas of your life.

My family talked about getting our chickens for months, as you would when adopting any pet. We chose their names carefully. Since they were girls and would offer us great nourishment, we thought to name them after goddesses. Our first batch of chickens arrived in a snow-storm; while the spring snow fell outside, my husband and daughter and I cuddled the two little peeping balls of fluff and pored through a book about goddesses in search of names.

> Every moment of our life is relationship. There is nothing except relationship. At this moment my relationship is to the rug, to the room, to my own body, to the sound of my voice.
>
> FROM *EVERYDAY ZEN*,
> CHARLOTTE JOKO BECK [18]

But names like Athena and Astarte seemed so lofty for these cute, bright-eyed babies. For our Easter Egger, we finally settled on Tara, which is short for Ostara, the Celtic Easter. She was tiny, brown, and a little too sleepy. The other chick that came that week we named Maisy, after a beloved character from a children's book who happens to be a mouse. We knew one of the chicks still to come would be a Rhode Island Red, so we named her Tallulah, after Maisy the mouse's red chicken friend. We were also expecting another chick to arrive, a Black Austrolorpe, whom we named Sylvie.

Tara continued to be too sleepy, a sign that something was wrong. I carried her around under my shirt to keep her warm, and gave her lots of healing Reiki energy. The next morning, though, she lay still, no longer breathing at all. We kept her little body in a paper bag until my husband got home from work, and then we three went out to bury her in the garden. It was my daughter's first experience of death. She seemed curious about it all until we got back in the house, when she burst into tears. I held her and we talked about how little Tara would always be a part of our family, resting in the garden beneath the lilacs.

The hatchery replaced Tara with another Easter Egger. We named our new hen Millie, after my grandmother. The next week, poor lonely Maisy, who would chirp frantically when left alone, got three mates. Maisy is still the more friendly of our hens, and we think this may be from that one week when we were her only companions and spent a lot of time holding and playing with her in the warm office. She bonded to us strongly, and we to her.

The three other babies who came shared Maisy's zest for life. Happily, we lost no more chicks. That early spring we spent a lot of time in the office, letting the perky babies out of their dog crate to explore. We wiped up a lot of teeny little droppings and made plans to have the carpet cleaned in the spring. But for then the office was chicken territory. While I worked at the computer, they cheeped at me to be let out.

I would turn to gaze at the crate to see little chicken heads peeking through the slats, hopeful that I might give up my work and come and play with them.

These chickens had become a part of our family, with names, personalities, and pecking order. We got to know them and they got to know us. As chicken ownership was new to us, we had to figure out the best ways to care for them. We were definitely beginners at the art of raising chickens.

CHICKEN DANCE

When our chickens finally went outside, it took us months to learn the chicken dance of what they wanted (to explore and scratch and peck), what we wanted (a not messy backyard), and how to set the boundaries. One day while doing yard work in front of our house, I realized Millie was happily trotting down the driveway toward the front yard. I tried to shoo her back up the driveway, but she dashed around me. I was very pregnant at the time and moved awkwardly. Unfortunately, I couldn't catch her.

HELP!" I YELLED out to my husband, throwing open the front door. "Millie's gotten out!"

My husband was indoors watching football on TV; I heard a slow shift from the sofa as I dashed off toward the neighbor's driveway, in hot pursuit of the newly escaped chicken.

Lowest in the pecking order, Millie tended to get to things last. But she was the first to figure out a way out of the yard through the gap behind the garage.

Chasing a chicken accomplishes quite the opposite of one's mission. She must be herded skillfully. This I was not doing. Instead my efforts were encouraging her to waddle-trot rapidly beyond our front yard and into the neighborhood. I made another poor attempt to shoo the hen back toward our garden while my husband, now emerged from the house, circled around on the sidewalk, his plastic flip-flops an echoing clap in the Sunday morning quiet. He ran up the far side of our neighbor's yard. Millie turned with a cluck and ran back toward me, dodging just before hitting the hedge between the houses. She realized her mistake only when she hit the fence, a dead end.

Chasing a chicken accomplishes quite the opposite of one's mission.

Or so I thought. But there was a chicken-sized gap between the gate and fence. Our oddly colored chicken's gray tail feathers waggled desperately until she popped through the space and into our neighbor's yard. Fortunately the gate was unlocked. My husband went through, scooped her up, and dropped her gently over the fence into our yard.

I scuttled off to patch up the gap behind the garage. Millie demonstrated her unsuspected intelligence by returning again and again to the spot where she had once gained her freedom.

I hammered up wire fencing, then tossed her back toward the yard. I attached another nail, then tossed her back toward the yard. Then another nail, and another toss. All rather awkwardly around my seven-month-pregnant belly. Millie never got out again. Nor, I might add, did any of the others.

A HOMESTEAD FOR CHICKENS

It seems that the art of raising chickens outside the farm is all about thinking on our toes. We have to learn from scratch, if you will, what will work in our little yards with our little flocks. People have been keeping chickens for 8,000 years, but they were doing it on farms, in villages, and at the edge of the wilderness. We do so in the city, in suburban or urban yards not designed for livestock. It was up to me to make ours so.

As I got to know my girls, I slowly got over my anxieties that the hens would escape or get sick or get eaten by the cats, who mostly ignored them. Our male cat is actually more of a "chicken" than our chickens; when I let the birds free-range, he won't go out in the backyard, but stares balefully from the door at the pecking ladies taking over his yard.

Take over the yard they did. I finally had a use for those black rain boots I bought years ago when volunteering at the organic farm. In Colorado, the ground is more often a dry rock than a muddy mess. Wearing my boots seemed a bit silly. In hot weather, in fact, they are unbearable, and so spend most of the gardening season sitting in storage. But now I had four poo-dropping machines who had evolved in cahoots with the land and therefore would deposit droppings haphazardly around the lawn. My grass loved the scattered nitrogen. It took me only one time of stepping in the natural fertilizer with bare feet to decide that I did not. One day I even sat on chicken poo, leaving a rather unsightly stain on a pair of khaki maternity pants.

It wasn't only their droppings that made a mess. Chickens provide a nice service to the land when they scratch at the dirt, churning the nitrogen into the soil and eliminating insects. After a day of chicken attentions, my compost heap would be flat, mulch was spread all over the lawn, baby salad leaves stood no chance. We decided letting the girls have free range all the time was not working in our suburban backyard.

We clipped a little door into the side of the chicken run, allowing them access to a corner of the yard that we surrounded with bird netting. While we still let them have free range of the whole yard every now and then as a treat, mostly they are contained in one corner of the yard. This is also true of their droppings and various scratchings. I also contained the compost heap, still the first place they go when we do let them out. Only now it isn't immediately flattened when we open the run door and let them roam free.

One day I saw Sylvie roaming around the yard when she was supposed to be contained in the pen. It turned out that the clever girls—or perhaps a conspiring squirrel—had snipped a hole in the hard-to-snip bird netting. Sylvie had found the hole and slipped through. I gathered her up and doubled the netting to help secure it more effectively. The next day, she got tangled up in the netting while attempting another escape. On a bad day, I might have become frustrated and questioned my sanity in bringing four sassy hens into our lives. But on this day, for whatever reason, my brilliant sanity (a Buddhist psychology term) was in full faculty. I carefully and mindfully untwisted the bird netting from my black chicken's greenish legs, repaired the hole, and smiled.

The chickens were teaching me both about hen husbandry and about my usual patterns of relating. You could say that they were teaching me hen zazen.

HEN ZAZEN

◆

In Zen Buddhism there is a practice called zazen, a sitting medita-
tion of coming into the present moment. "Zazen practice," says Suzu-
ki-roshi, "is the direct expression of our true nature. Strictly speak-
ing, for a human being, there is no other practice than this practice;
there is no other way of life than this life." [19] *He means that coming*
into the present moment, being here now, without getting caught up
in the future or the past (which exists only in our thoughts), is the
goal of spiritual practice or zazen.

THE TRADITIONAL POSTURE of zazen is sitting in full lotus
with your spine straight, your hands resting in your lap,
your chin tucked, and your crown pressing up toward the sky.
Zazen can also be practiced standing or walking. Or, in the
case of hen zazen, watching your chickens.

When we first let our pullets outside, I followed them
around as they explored their new yard. Having only had the
carpet of our office to scratch at, they were thrilled. Grass!
Soil! Real insects! Though tens of thousands of years of
chicken genes told them what to do (scratch, check soil,
repeat), they had never encountered such a world. They were
in beginner's mind. Since a chicken is rarely distracted by her
thoughts as far as I know, for her, entering beginner's mind is
not terribly difficult. Projecting myself through their eyes, I
was able to enter beginner's mind as well. I saw my backyard

anew. I noticed the sounds of the neighborhood as if hearing them for the first time. I noticed the breeze ruffling Maisy's peach-colored feathers and the sun shining off Sylvie's black back, turning it opalescent green. I came into the present moment, just being with my new chickens. I observed myself, and I observed them. This is hen zazen.

Have you ever really noticed how inconsequential our thoughts are? I don't mean the "big" thoughts that can lead to action and therefore have a bearing on reality. I mean 95 percent of the thoughts going through your mind moment to moment. We chatter on with lists of things to do, the conversations that might happen, a litany of complaints, and all manner of self-talk. Meditation is to these thoughts what a chicken is to a bare spot of soil: just as she will scratch at the surface to uncover the truth below, meditation illuminates what we hide beneath the surface even from ourselves. As you

> To me chickens are beautiful creatures and relaxing to watch. I love looking out my window and seeing them bustle around the yard. They have an interesting social structure and, contrary to popular opinion, are quite smart. They are constantly busy, a state to which I can easily relate.
>
> FROM *THE COMPLETE CHICKEN*, PAM PERCY [20]

sit and watch your breath, you see before you the constant and nearly useless *thinking* that goes on. You realize you just don't need those thoughts in order to be *you*.

The ego loves its thoughts. Complaints, lists, repetition, and desires make up the ego's castle. Begin to notice the castle walls, and you begin to see that in fact the castle is a facade. The ego, however, does not want you to notice this, any more than an insect in the soil wants a chicken to come do her little dance on his house. To mix metaphors, your mind is a busy chicken scratching at the mulch. If you're like me, you think that if you just *think* about something long enough, you will work it out. Occasionally this is true. Usually, however, it is in the pause of thought, the moving on to other things, that light is shed on whatever it was that needed illuminating. Like when you stop trying to remember the title of that song or the name of your friend's boss, and it flashes into your head.

In truth, most of what we do throughout the day requires little or no thought. Driving, bathing the baby, feeding the chickens, even writing the shopping list require no active thinking on your part. We just do our tasks. Thoughts may arise, but we don't need them in order to know that we should, say, rub soap into the baby's hair, or put eggs into the shopping cart. This isn't to say that you are mindlessly going about your tasks; if you can notice your thoughts and step free of them, you are practicing mindfulness, not mindlessness. All it takes is noticing. This is zazen, too.

Next time you catch yourself thinking something to death, picture in your mind a chicken scratching away. Laugh at yourself, take a deep breath, and let the thoughts go. It may be easier said than done, but I notice that, when I can find something to laugh at, everything looks and feels much better. Life goes on.

Watching chickens is a very old human pastime, and the forerunner of psychology, sociology, and management theory. Sometimes understanding yourself can be made easier by projection on to others. Watching chickens helps us understand human motivations and interactions, which is doubtless why so many words and phrases in common parlance are redolent of the hen yard: "pecking order," "cockiness," "ruffling somebody's feathers," "taking somebody under your wing," "fussing like a mother hen," "strutting," a "bantamweight fighter," "clipping someone's wings," "beady eyes," "chicks," "to crow," "to flock," "to get in a flap," "coming home to roost," "don't count your chickens before they're hatched," "nest eggs," and "preening."

PETER LENNOX, *TIMES HIGHER EDUCATION,* [21]

BASIC GOODNESS OF THE CHICKEN

My chickens have taught me about myself, by being valued pets, by inviting me into the practice of chicken husbandry, and by slowing me down to witness their chicken-centered antics. They are a valuable part of my spiritual practice simply by being both a unique and an everyday part of my life. They are "nothing special" and they are a wholly different way of living on the land. They teach me about being present and offer the simple but profound lessons of companionship.

COMPANION MEANS FRIEND, someone we are with. Chickens ask nothing of us except a warm, clean place to sleep, and some treats every now and then (crickets and mealworms are best, but leftover cabbage will do). Mostly, though, they peck and scratch and go about their business. We, as owners, project all sorts of thoughts about how they are enlightened or stupid, but really they are just exhibiting their basic essence. This is why they can be good meditation instructors. But since they are loved pets who ask little of us but our presence, they can also offer a little pet therapy.

Pets lower our levels of stress, improve our sense of well-being, and enhance our quality of life. Animals have been successfully used in physical and behavioral therapy for children and adults. People who keep pets have lower stress levels and lower blood pressure. In one study, researchers found that the presence of a pet was "more effective than that

Cindy Anderson suffers from dysautonomia, the
disregulation of the autonomic nervous system,
which controls organ function. She takes one day at
a time, trying to stay positive through the physical
and financial challenges of everyday life. One of the
biggest blessings for her is her backyard flock of
eighteen chickens and one rooster. She said,
"I have been going through a lot of things since
being diagnosed with a pretty debilitating disease
[including] depression and the inability to do anything
really strenuous … I am finding that the chickens are
really good therapy for me … My family and friends
have all remarked at how happy I am lately. They
haven't seen that in me for about seven years. I also
find a spiritual calm in my chickens. For me finding
a way to find meaning in life is important. With
chickens I see the full circle of life … Birth to
death … I have never felt closer to my higher power
(as I understand that to mean) than I do now."

FROM "HUMAN-ANIMAL BONDS," FROMA WALSH [22]

of a spouse or friend in ameliorating the cardiovascular effects
of stress." [23] It is interesting to note that these are similar
effects to those of regular meditation.

The pets used in pet therapy and studies of pet–human interactions are usually cats and dogs. But chickens, because of their unique personalities and ability to interact directly with a person, can provide the same benefits.

> Jana Clairmont of Polson, Montana, regularly brings her rooster Alex and her Cornish game hen Carlita to local schools, rehabilitation centers, and retirement homes. She calls her volunteer chicken-therapy practice Fowl Play. She says, "Most of your seniors were raised around chickens and cows. Holding … a chicken can bring back memories for older people." Children love handling the birds, too.
>
> FROM "FEATHERED FRIENDS," FROMA WALSH [24]

Pets or animal companions offer us windows into our own basic goodness. Basic goodness is the underlying sanity, gentleness, and wisdom that we all possess, which we try to access through spiritual practice and especially meditation. It is part of our essence, as it is in the chicken or any other creature. By caring for our chickens, we encounter our basic goodness in the mirror of another. In developing compassion for another, we are able to be more compassionate toward ourselves, which is one of the foundations of health.

ATTUNING WITH CHICKENS

When the girls were a few months old, they began laying eggs—and announced said eggs each morning with a loud bawk-bawk-bawk-BAWK. I dearly hoped the neighbors wouldn't care. Strictly speaking, our local regulations don't allow for chickens. If someone complained, we would have to get rid of our four hens. So when they started advertising their pride and joy, or bickering over who got the nest box next, I would run out to the coop and shush them by tossing treats into the pen. I worried about rewarding their squawking, but it seemed to work. They would hush. After a time they seemed to grow out of the annoying habit. So when I heard a strange squawking coming from the coop in the middle of the day, I knew something must be amiss.

Juliet, an Ancona chicken, was weak as a chick,
unable to even hold up her head. Depite this, she
had such a huge will to live, and a huge appetite, that
she survived even though she was unable to walk.
Her owner, a ten-year-old girl, has cerebral palsy
and uses crutches or a walker to move around.
She and Juliet bonded instantly and they spend all
their time together.

WWW.BACKYARDCHICKENS.COM [25]

I WENT OUT TO the yard with the intention of shutting them up. To my surprise, they were all out in the external run, not in the coop or the aviary where they usually did their song and dance. Maisy, top chicken, was doing the bawking. She stood a little away from the bushes that line their pen. The other three huddled under the greenery. I had never seen such behavior from them.

Then movement on the telephone pole at the back of their pen caught my eye; a Cooper's hawk took flight as soon as I neared the coop. Cooper's hawks love eating smaller birds. A female can actually catch a pigeon mid-flight. This one thought she might try a little chicken dinner, never mind that our pullets were equal to her in weight and twice her girth.

I scared away the hawk, but what impressed me most was Maisy's bravery in protecting her little family. Her cry seemed a combination of battle cry, warning, and call for help. I knew right away that her call meant danger, even though I had never heard it before and it sounded very similar to the egg squawk. I was learning their language. I was attuning to my birds. In doing so I was attuning to the environment as well.

A special synergy happens when you spend extended periods of time with animals. Though I was aware of this connection with cats and dogs, I had never before felt it with birds. If a year earlier someone had told me that I would become attuned to the language of my chickens, I might have laughed in their face. I didn't know they did more than cluck. Now I know it is not only possible, but likely. All it takes is attention, and the attunement takes care of itself. In time we learn to speak a language without words.

Allowing our Witness to Function

All of these stories, from therapy chickens to hen zazen and learning the language of your birds, are about getting to know chickens through observation and affinity. These stories can be models for our own ability to "witness," or to watch ourselves interacting with what is. Meditation, spiritual practice, and even chicken husbandry can all teach us about "witnessing." While

All of these stories ... are about getting to know chickens through observation and affinity.

we can become involved emotionally with chickens, healing, gardening, whatever, we can also take all of these moments in our lives to step back and allow our Witness to function. The Tibetan Lama, Tarthang Tulku, writes, "When you face the 'watcher' directly, your awareness and the 'watcher' become one. There is no self to watch anything. There is only watching, only the process. There is no subject and object. The process is the experience ... or you could say, pure awareness." [26]

That moment when you are no longer attached to your thoughts is pure awareness. I find this space when gardening or watching my chickens. Also sometimes when washing the dishes, rocking a baby to sleep, watching light on water ...

you will have your own moments when you will settle into the deep stillness behind the chattering mind. From that pool of stillness you can watch or witness your thoughts—they do not stop, but keep rolling like a ticker tape—and become wholly your deeper self. This is something that's hard to write about, but is so basically simple when you get there.

Here is a way to find that place. Sit outside with your chickens. Watch them. Notice your breath. Just watch them. Notice what they notice. Feel the earth beneath you, the air around you, any tension in your body. Keep watching your chickens. At the same time, observe yourself, just noticing what is, breathing, watching. Becoming aware. This may sound silly, hen zazen, but try it. See what happens.

Notice. Now ask yourself: Who is aware?

> To my mind, the idea that doing dishes is unpleasant can occur only when you aren't doing them. Once you are standing in front of the sink with your sleeves rolled up and your hands in the warm water, it is really quite pleasant. I enjoy taking my time with each dish, being fully aware of the dish, the water, and each movement of my hands ...
> The dishes themselves and the fact that I am here washing them are miracles!
>
> FROM *PEACE IS EVERY STEP*, THICH NHAT HANH [27]

When you enter into the space of the Witness into pure awareness, and maybe your thoughts keep going separately from your identity, you can experience something like vertigo. You startle yourself back into identification with your thoughts. That's okay—just notice when this happens. Notice any fear or shame or doubt that arises. Notice yourself. Notice what is. Notice yourself noticing. Who is noticing? Who is aware? These bits of clarity into your self and the world form the foundations of sanity and enlightenment.

CHICKEN JOURNAL

Study your relationship with anything deeply, and you will discover much about yourself and the world. You may find it valuable to keep a journal relating to your chickens, documenting your unique relationship with these special birds. Recording your thoughts about them, your insights into hen zazen, as well as some simple details about their care will show you much about how you relate to your animals and how they relate to you. Remember: your life is your practice.

WRITE IN YOUR JOURNAL, draw in your journal, and let your journal-keeping be your practice. It can be part baby (chicken) book, part farmer's almanac, and part spiritual memoir. Here are a few writing prompts to get you started:

- Why did you decide to raise chickens? What concerns did you have? How did you address these concerns?

- Tell the story of bringing your chicks home. Where did they stay? How did other family members relate to them?

- Do you have a special bond with one of your birds? Write about that relationship and what it has taught you.

- What challenges have you dealt with in raising hens? What has this taught you about other parts of your life?

- What do others (neighbors, children, family members) think of your raising chickens? Are they envious? Think you're a little crazy? Just curious?

- Spend some time just sitting and watching the birds in the yard. Record your observations and your thoughts. Notice what happens if you enter into pure awareness.

- What is the funniest thing a chicken has done? Tell the story using as many sensory details as you can.

Include in your journal drawings and photographs, dates and details (such as the first egg, when molting happens, and so on), maybe a feather or two, even bird prints! Muddy chicken feet on watercolor paper could make a fun bit of art for your journal. Perhaps include official documents such as licenses, articles from your local paper about chickens, and contact information for vets, other owners, and local clubs.

Your chicken journal can be a work of art and play. Your journal is your own, so it can be as light-hearted, creative, serious, or spiritual as you like. It is a record of your unique relationship with your unique birds. And since all is relationship, it is a record of your spiritual path, your life, your relationship, ultimately, with yourself. Let this chicken journal be a project that leads you to discover yourself.

THE SUCH-NESS OF CHICKENS

So what is it about this relationship that leads us to a spiritual relationship with ourselves and the Divine? Chickens are funny, awkward, beautiful, earthy—not really what one would call spiritual. That, in fact, is what makes them a perfect focus for the practice that is your life. Their unapologetic, unselfconscious, funny, awkward beauty pecks us right into beginner's mind. We can forget what it means to "be spiritual" and just live life. Through the realness of birth and death, the every-moment-ness of the chicken, we stop and become our real selves. We enter a conscious relationship with what is.

IN BUDDHISM the word 'such-ness' is used to mean 'the essence or particular characteristics of a thing or person, its true nature.' Each person has his or her such-ness," [28] writes Thich Nhat Hanh. The such-ness of the chicken brings us into our own such-ness, our own brilliant sanity. With chickens,

what you see is what you get. They are curious, determined, all more or less present and accounted for. They live to follow the patterns of the chicken: rise, lay, peck, scratch, take a dirt bath. Right here, in front of you, is life. Keep the coop clean, gather the eggs, provide fresh water, corn, and insects. These practices can provide insight into the such-ness of life, without the layers of suffering that we paste over every little step. Then all becomes sacred, even the chicken and our care of our flock.

Writes psychotherapist John Welwood, "As soon as we look beyond both duty and pleasure for a deeper meaning and purpose in relationship today, we start to move in the direction of the sacred, which we could define as coming *into deeper connection with our true, essential nature* [his italics], behind all our masks and facades."[30] He is referring to the intimate relationship between two humans, but his words offer us some insight into why chickens can actually offer us an entry point into spiritual awakening—and why raising a little flock of chickens for companionship and eggs can actually be a sacred practice. The art of raising chickens today, when it is more than just a simple survival measure but is a political act and a vote for compassionate living, is part of our move for deeper meaning

> Birth to death ... I have never felt closer to my higher power (as I understand that to mean) than I do now.
>
> CINDY ANDERSON, CHICKEN OWNER [29]

and purpose. Raising chickens as a relationship—with chickens, the land, our community—reflects on our sacred relationship with ourselves. With Life. With a Higher Power, whether that be God or Goddess or our own Buddha Nature. No facade, just ourselves, coming into deeper connection with our true essential nature.

Partly because raising chickens allows us just to be ourselves—chickens ask nothing more of us—we enter into a space of sacred relationship with our inner self. As I gather the eggs and pet a bird who peers at me with lovely orange eyes, I breathe more deeply. I inhabit my body. I inhabit my natural self, if you will. I just am. I inhabit my such-ness. The such-ness of chickens becomes a mirror; in them we are able to observe the such-ness of ourselves. So then the very act of moving, breathing, interacting with chickens, the land, our family, becomes a meditation.

> All is relationship.
> Your practice is your life.
> There is no other way of life than this, to be aware.
> To enter beginner's mind.
> *Who is aware?*

CHAPTER THREE

CHOP WOOD, FEED CHICKENS

Often those of us who keep hens also garden, like to fix and build things ourselves, and might keep goats, bees, or other animals as well. We might be into knitting or sewing, making yogurt and cheese, collecting gray water for the flower patch, or living off the grid. We aspire toward greater self-sufficiency and a smaller carbon footprint. Hobby farmers—whether we are largely self-sufficient and living far from any city, or practicing a few traditional skills on an urban plot— share a view of nature as sacred or part of divinity. Through our relationship with the sacred land, we develop greater mindfulness through the marvelous actions that make up our lives.

HOME, HOME ON THE HOBBY FARM

◆

One spring day, after a lingering, cold winter, I got up early. While my husband held the baby and cooked breakfast, and our daughter played games on the computer, I went outside to let out the chickens. The air was cool, the ground frozen solid. Frost rimmed each blade of grass, brown leaf, and mulch mound. I sucked in my breath, letting the cool damp into my lungs. The chickens called restlessly from inside the coop. I opened the run door, opened the coop, and greeted each feathered lady as she headed down the ramp.

I GATHERED A BUCKET, fresh shavings, and gloves from the garage. Neighborhood dogs barked at squirrels and a plane flew through the pale blue sky. With the girls crooning curiously behind me, I scooped soiled shavings into the bucket. I dumped the litter on an unplanted garden bed. My ego, my "self," sat quietly as I moved in harmony with the sun, the spring earth, and our hens. I practiced, without any mental effort, the meditations of urban hobby farming.

> Magical Power,
>   marvelous action!
> Chopping wood,
>   carrying water …
> SOIKU SIGEMATSU [31]

As we saw in the previous chapter, simply attuning to your awareness while spending time with your hens can bring you into a meditative state. The same is true of all hobby farm chores. Even more so, the actions of hobby farming address an even larger network of meaning while giving us more opportunity to step outside the ego and into our larger self. We are hobby farmers because we care about the earth, our communities, and our families. We want to live closer to an "ideal" life, one that interacts with the earth while leaving less of a trace of our actions. In turn,

> [Hobby farming is a story] of quest and rebirth as old lives and "mainstream" culture are left behind, of pursuing a spiritual life but not in a formal religious setting, of recentering the self amid the wonders (and resources) of the natural world.
>
> FROM *AT HOME IN NATURE*, REBECCA KNEALE GOULD [32]

these very actions teach us deeper compassion for ourselves, the earth, and all our relations, from humans to hens to hellebores.

In 1854, the American author Henry David Thoreau published *Walden*. His work inspired a back-to-the-land movement based on living with nature as spiritual guide. For the next hundred years, hobby farmers moved away from the city for their Good Life, seeking meaning via self-cultivation in the context of sacred nature. In the last few decades, hobby farming has seen a transition of sorts as the ideals of centering one's life around home, doing for oneself, and honoring the land moved back into urban and suburban settings. Hobby farming has for many become less about divorcing oneself from technology and the city, and more about finding a center at home and leading a considerably more balanced life.

City hobby farmers argue that we can have it all: provide for some of our own survival, live a creative life, and enjoy the bustle and benefit of a larger community. For this reason urban hobby farming is about hope, the hope that we can craft a dynamic, integrated, and sustainable way of life on earth.

I raise some of my own food, do basic repairs on my house myself, compost and otherwise reduce my waste output where I can, and rely on my community for many additional resources such as clothing. But, though we have gotten rid of our television, we regard a high-speed Internet connection to be a necessity. I cook most of our meals, but enjoy eating out or ordering in several times a month. I can sew my own clothes, but I enjoy shopping at thrift stores, which saves time while reducing my spending and also reusing resources, both key tenets of hobby farming. I am far from being a zealot about frugal living and doing for myself, but I am rather zealous about the practices of gardening, raising chickens, and living a green lifestyle. Urban hobby farming is about balance, taking what works for your family and living all things in moderation.

SELF-SUFFICIENT HOBBY FARMING

People are hungry for hobby farming skills, especially in the city. In the midst of our high-tech lives, we all long for balance. We want to be self-sufficient and also live close to our city jobs, such as my

husband's job as a music therapist at a large children's hospital to which he can cycle. We want to be able to walk to a nice, trendy coffee shop and then gather the used grinds to sprinkle on the garden beds at home. We want to marry the city to the country, a career to a home, self-sufficiency to an interconnected neighborhood.

THE MARRIAGE OF WORLDS is a healthy development of an evolving society, leading to balance in our lives and the integration of our inner selves. The urban hobby farm gives one a chance to come home to oneself, all of oneself, in exactly the ways that work for you and your family. It's also an exciting way to build a new society of interconnected yet self-sufficient people.

Rebecca Kneale Gould, student of religion and history, studied "homesteaders," or hobby farmers, in her book *At Home in Nature: Modern Homesteading and Spiritual Practice in America*. She found that they "share a common commitment to on-the-ground environmental ethics, do-it-yourself pragmatics, and an improvisational, nature-based spiritual practice." [33]

In other words, we want to live in connection with the sacred land through our daily lives. We also want a community that shares our ideals and understands our struggles. Building community is a key part of hobby farming. Often community grows around tasks, such as candle-making or building a straw bale house. Hobby farming is about providing for your own survival, such as building your own house, creating a gray-

> A life of hobby farming ritualizes a complex relationship with nature, one in which nature is placed at the center of life as the source of meaning and authority.
>
> FROM *AT HOME IN NATURE*,
> REBECCA KNEALE GOULD [34]

water pond, or knitting a sweater—and growing your own food. Urban hobby farming differs from back-to-the-land hobby farming in that we tend not to build our own homes or live fully off the grid (though we may be able to do so somewhat by installing solar panels and doing our own remodeling), but providing for at least some of our own food is part of our pragmatism. Food production is a central part of urban hobby farming. Home-grown food in an urban setting might include:

- **A vegetable garden**
- **Fruit trees and bushes**
- **Bees**
- **Pygmy goats**
- **Cheese-making**
- **Bottling and preserving**
- **A frost-free root cellar or basement to store food**
- **And, of course, chickens.**

Not all of these work for, or appeal to, everyone. One aspect that makes raising chickens so appealing to the aspiring urban hobby farmer is the relative ease of their care. For

someone with physical challenges, for instance, tending an acre of garden or backyard may be too difficult. Feeding and watering a small flock of birds, brushing out their coop once a week, and gathering eggs can be more accessible.

CHICKENS TO FIT YOUR LIFE

Keeping hens is an ideal introduction to urban hobby farming. A small flock is easy to care for, and can fit into the urbanite's busy lifestyle. Once you have set up your coop and run, and the young pullets can go outside, chickens require about as much care as cats. Here are a few suggestions for fitting chickens into a busy lifestyle.

BECAUSE WE THINK of farm animals as requiring lots of work, it can be surprising to realize that raising hens is fairly easy. Once you get used to your birds, you will find that keeping them is so easy, in fact, that it will encourage you to live a more laid-back lifestyle.

For us the initial hurdles were where to get chicks, how to keep them safe as babies, how to build our coop, and where to buy feed and supplies. After the initial phase of planning and set-up was over, we worked out the best routine for caring for our chickens. Since I was pregnant that first spring and summer, cleaning out the coop fell to my husband. Whichever of us was up in the morning would go out to open

the coop, which we keep locked at night. I stay home with the children, so it was usually up to me or our preschool-age daughter to feed and water them once during the day. Then when my husband came home from work, he usually locked up the chickens for the night, putting their food and water into the coop before shutting the door. This way we would not attract rats or other predators. The chickens' care is manageable around a work schedule. Most work schedules also fit the chickens' schedules, since they wake with the sun and go to bed when it gets dark.

Our coop and aviary are small, taking up about 30 sq. ft. (3 m^2), so we use the smallest food and water system we can. We still use the same water bottle and feeder we bought for our chicks, since they are small and portable. We put them in the coop at night and pull them out during the day. Larger waterers and feeders take up more space but require less maintenance.

Part of the fun of keeping chickens is interacting with them and caring for them. I recommend, therefore, assigning duties to the family members who can most easily carry them out; for example, children gathering eggs after school and the adult who works outside the home tucking the chickens in just as he or she gets home. My childhood friends who had chickens learned only when they were older just how their mother Fran had arranged to involve them

> *Part of the fun of keeping chickens is interacting with them and caring for them.*

in the care of the hens. The three children went to different schools and would arrive home at different times. When Fran's youngest arrived home, she would send the little girl out to gather eggs. Then while her daughter played, Fran would secretly return the eggs to the coop. Her middle child came home then, and would be sent out for her daily egg-gathering chore. While this daughter watched a television program, Fran would again return the eggs to the coop in preparation for the eldest, who would then gather the eggs a third time. Everyone felt involved and busy, and the eggs were very thoroughly gathered.

> **The Red Wheelbarrow**
>
> so much depends
> upon
>
> a red wheel
> barrow
>
> glazed with rain
> water
>
> beside the white
> chickens.
>
> WILLIAM CARLOS WILLIAMS, 1923

THE CENTERED HOME

◆

Urban hobby farming, creating family-based greater self-sufficiency through gardening, do-it-yourself projects, and small-scale animal husbandry, is one way to create a healthy home. Raising your food, attending to animals, and practicing other forms of self-sufficiency is to your home what a deep breath is to your body. You come fully into your own space. Your energy is centered here, at home. For not only is nature sacred to the hobby farmer, but so is the home itself.

TRY THIS HOME MEDITATION to understand the spiritual aspect of the physical space of your home. Take a deep breath. Center yourself in your own body. Feel your breath move in and out of your lungs. Notice what you learn, of what you are aware, simply by breathing. Now imagine your breath moves through your entire home. See your breath move into your body, then out into your home. Then let your entire home breathe with you as the center. Breathe for a few moments, feeling this wind move through the house. Notice what you become aware of. Let your breath expand to fill the land your house sits on. Notice what is happening. What do you feel? What does your home tell you?

This may seem like an odd exercise if you are not used to sensing beyond yourself. Try it every day for a few moments just to center yourself in your body and your home. Try some house-breathing while you do the dishwashing or take a shower after gathering eggs. You will find that images, feelings, or phrases come into your awareness that tell you something about the health of your home environment. You will become aware of spots of stagnant energy, places where energy moves too fast—like a line of doorways—and other areas that need your attention. Attending to these areas by de-cluttering, reorganizing, cleaning, and repairing will affect your health and the health of all who share your home with you. Including your chickens. Everything is connected and everything is energy, including homes and yards and those who live there.

For hobby farming resources in your area try:

- *www.backyardchickens.com*—Offers a wealth of information on coop-building, chicken breeds, and hen care. Also includes a large, active forum.
- *www.backyardpoultrymag.com*—Contains a vast resource library pertaining to poultry care, as well as a bookstore, breeders' directory, and more.
- *www.urbanchickens.org*—Contains a blog and forum, chicken-care pages, information of chicken-keeping ordinances and laws, and a further resource page.
- *www.hobbyfarms.com*—Features a newsletter, a hobby farm community, and ideas and resources for sustainable living.
- *www.motherearthnews.com*—The "original guide to living wisely," this magazine's website contains thousands of articles on homesteading and green living.

One of the concerns of local councils in making urban chicken ownership legal is that chickens are messy and chicken coops an eyesore. This need not be so. In fact, the number-one way to keep your hens healthy is to keep their coop and run clean. Changing the shavings and straw regularly, making sure your chickens have fresh water and food, and regularly cleaning up their droppings keep your birds healthy and your backyard looking nice. Attending to their food and water

reduces the risk of rats and other vermin infesting the area. Containing their droppings in a well-tended compost heap keeps the yard healthy and happy, too.

The same is true of your home. We must keep our homes literally and spiritually fresh. Our homes reflect us. They are extensions of our inner world, of our minds and spirits. Keep them clean, in and out, and you create health for the entire organism, including you, your chickens, and the world beyond.

This home meditation will teach you where there are stuck spots that need attention, and as you become more proficient, you may be alerted to threatening illness among family members, or in your hens, before it arises. It will also offer you suggestions for ways in which you can center more deeply at home through further hobby farming practices.

> [Hobby farming] means staying at home but in the richest possible sense.
>
> FROM *AT HOME IN NATURE*,
> REBECCA KNEALE GOULD [35]

Whenever I work in the yard, I like to dream about the next development in the landscape. I do this by feeling into the yard and asking it what it wants to express. When my first child was born, we saved her placenta and planted it under an apple tree. With my second child, I knew I wanted to repeat the practice, but was unsure as to what plant I would add to the yard. I sat on the patio and breathed with the yard, letting my eye-focus soften and my intuitive feelers spread out. Several ideas came to mind. As I practiced this meditation

repeatedly over several months, the strongest pull was to plant raspberries near my fence. Each time I meditated with the yard and garden on the idea of raspberries, the concept became clearer. My son's first spring, we put in a patch of raspberries.

THE URBAN HOBBY FARMER'S COMMUNITY

Hobby farming is an attitude, not a set of rules. Your hobby farming will differ from mine, depending on your skill level, value system, family needs, and local resources. Whether you are rural or urban, community resources form an integral part of your hobby farm. This is especially true in urban hobby farms where a network of resources— local farmers, artisans, and friends—create the farm.

I INVITED A GROUP of mothers to gather with our home-schooled children and learn hobby farming skills such as making candles, bottling, gardening, and raising chickens. Everyone was very interested and excited, offering ideas and energy. Several mothers traveled an hour to our first gathering, at which we made candles. Some home-schooled their children, and others did not. The group included people of diverse ethnicities, income levels, spiritual paths, and careers. Our similarities included living in the same metropolitan area and wanting to raise well-attached children in balanced, natural ways. These mothers believed that children who know

> Dig! Dig! Dig! And your
> muscles will grow big
> Keep on pushing the spade
> Don't mind the worms
> Just ignore their squirms
> And when your back aches,
> laugh with glee
> And keep on diggin'
> Till we give our foes a Wiggin'
> Dig! Dig! Dig! to Victory.
>
> WWII Dig for Victory Anthem [36]

how to raise their own food and craft their own things will grow up to be well-rounded adults. One of the mothers who joined us also raises chickens, trading her extra eggs for credit at a local cafe. Other mothers sew, knit, or garden, and many would like to raise chickens. They and their children gathered outside our coop to watch the hens, who crooned curiously in the hope of treats. We then took turns in my tiny kitchen to melt old candles and new beeswax, and then pour the liquid wax into bottles and molds. The children played, and the mothers drank coffee and talked.

On another day my family loaded up the bike trailer and rode the few miles to a local farmers' market. Local vendors sold coffee, popcorn, and vegetables. An accordionist played Disney tunes. A local music school invited children to try their hands at playing an electric keyboard. My favorite vendor was a young couple who grew rare heirloom vegetables in their suburban garden where the plots of land are tiny. The Japanese eggplants and zebra-striped tomatoes did well in their organic raised beds. They were able to grow some of their food and sell the extra at the market.

My mothers' group regularly organizes co-operatives of combined purchasing power. We order dried herbs, organic home products such as cleaners, and even whole cows. One co-operative ordered so much meat that it ended up grounding a plane on the west side of the mountains because it was so heavy. The meat eventually arrived, was divided up, and was stored in freezers across the city.

In his blog "Hen Waller," urban farmer Patrick writes about his community's annual Tomato ExtravaCanza, where a group of friends get together to can 130 lbs. (60 kg) of tomatoes in the hope that they will not have to purchase any sauce from the store over the winter. He writes, "The 130 pounds of tomatoes yielded 1.4 pounds [per pint], or about 94 pints of tomatoes. [My wife] Holly and I are taking much of that for our pantry. Will it be enough? Only time will tell." [37]

My hobby farm depends on my community. I found my community online, though I meet regularly "in real life" with some of the mothers in my online group. One of the beauties of hobby farming in the modern age is that we do have the Internet as a resource. The Internet connects like-minded people who seek to create healthy homes and communities by staying at home. Rather than eschewing available technological resources, we hobby farmers can make our hobby farms stronger by utilizing them. When used wisely, the Internet is part of our community and an easily available research tool. Online, one can find information about local farmers' markets, community gardens, forums such as backyardchick ens.com, and techniques such as biodynamic farming or per-maculture. Another tool for connecting with your local community is magazines. Magazines such as *Mother Earth News*, *Urban Farms*, and *Back Home Magazine*, to name just a few avail-able in the U.S., all offer resources, ideas, and ways to connect with other like-minded individuals.

Hobby farming communities that are focused on the desire to live more meaningful, earth-friendly lives are literally shaping a new world from the ground up. Our lawns and parking lots are being broken up, and vegetable gardens put in. Legislature is changing to meet the strong desire for a home- and healthy-food-based society. In the U.S. and Canada, community gardens are run locally, usually by non-profit or community associations. There are more community gardens every year as the desire for food-based community surges, and cities themselves are helping to unite and support com-munity gardens. In the UK, 300,000 people have allotments, but the demand for more land and more gardens outstrips supply. The UK government has created the Community Land Bank in co-operation with the Federation of City Farms and Community Gardens to meet this need.

The same is true of farmers' markets, which are far from new, but fell out of common practice as food sales became the jurisdiction of supermarkets. Farmers' markets are one of the oldest forms of direct marketing by small farmers. From the traditional "mercados" in the Peruvian Andes to Asia's unique street markets, growers all over the world gather weekly to sell their produce directly to the public. "In the last decade, they have become a favorite marketing method for many farmers ... and weekly ritual for many shoppers," says the Local Harvest website.[38] Those shoppers, gardeners, and small-scale farmers will renew our culture by bringing us back down to earth.

CHANGING THE WORLD

What does the advent of the Internet, the resurgence of local markets, and the demand for community gardens say about our changing society? Hobby farming is a spiritual process of self-cultivation and reconnecting with the sacred land. The resurgence on a broad cultural level of a hobby farming paradigm speaks of a cross-cultural spiritual awakening. The World War II campaigns of Victory Gardens in the U.S. and Dig for Victory in the UK were about supporting the war effort. In contrast, the hobby farming movement comes not from any sense of fear and conquest, but from compassion. And as such, it is helping to create a world built on this love.

I DREAM OF A WORLD where every garden grows a little food, where every flat rooftop, corner plot, and park boasts an organic garden. Where a little flock of chickens is seen as prosperity—not just financial but spiritual prosperity. Where

all our children grow up knowing the sacred land. Knowing where Brussels sprouts come from. Knowing how soft a chicken's feathers are and the sound of a hen's croon. Can you imagine what such a world would look like?

I believe strongly in the power of creative visualization and manifestation. I recently looked back at journals of mine that I had written years ago. In them, I had listed my dreams in detail. They included healthy children, a happy marriage, a lovely home, and, yes, a flock of chickens. Today, almost ten years later, these dreams are now realities. We can create the individual and collective worlds of which we dream by visualizing them and then taking steps to make them happen.

> We are worried about pollution and litter. People can learn about farms and how to care for them and not be so selfish.
>
> HIRZA MAHMOOD, AGED 11,
> QUOTED ON
> WWW.FARMGARDEN.ORG.UK

Just as you breathed into your home and land, let us take a moment to breathe into the world.

When practicing this form of meditation, it is extremely important that you first ground and center yourself firmly. You can do this by feeling the weight of your body on the earth or seeing roots of light grow from your base into the ground beneath you. Breathe into these roots. Breathe into the solid ground below. Feel the sensations inside your body to center you. Take some time grounding and centering before and after this meditation.

Now close your eyes and feel your awareness expand beyond your body. Take in your home with your awareness and your breath. Grow to encompass your neighborhood. Take your time to do this. Now expand your focus to include your city. Keep going until you can breathe with your country, then the continent, and then the planet.

The first time you do this, take your time. It can be totally overwhelming to feel the entire planet. Awareness can also be liberating: you are so much bigger than yourself. We are all one. Keep breathing. Come back to the sensations in your body any time you feel too vast. Anchor yourself in your body.

When you are feeling ready, visualize the interconnections of a compassionate world in which each person is rooted at home, anchored to his or her self, providing for some of his or her food, clothing, and home. See the routes that our food travels. See the pathways of lovingly crafted materials such as clothing, furniture, musical instruments, and even computers, cell phones, and satellites. Keep breathing. What kind of world shall we create?

> [The] practice of [smallholding] continually articulated an attempt to live a good and moral life, a life that might redeem society or at least the self.
>
> FROM *AT HOME IN NATURE*, REBECCA KNEALE GOULD [39]

Come back to yourself by breathing into your hara, or center of energy, in your belly. Focus your attention on your body. Feel the vibrations in your hands and feet. Feel the

weight of your seat on the floor or chair. Come back to your center, the sacred center that is your body. Come home. If you feel dizzy after this meditation, try eating something, drinking a hot drink, or simply sitting on the earth. Sit with your back to a tree and let her teach you how to ground.

> The awakening to our true self is the awakening to that entirety [of the whole world], breaking out of the prison-self of separate ego. The one who perceives this is the bodhisattva—and we are all bodisattvas because we are all capable of experiencing that—it is our true nature.
>
> FROM "THE GREENING OF THE SELF," JOANNA MACY [40]

BEYOND THE CHICKEN

I didn't feel like I could call my suburban home a hobby farm until I expanded beyond the vegetable garden by adding chickens. Including food-producing animals on my land not only gave me protein from my backyard, but it closed a loop. Now our care for the land gives us vegetables, fruits, and eggs. Much of our food waste goes back to the land as compost, chicken food, and, subsequently, chicken manure. Chickens are a lovely and easy way to settle into a hobby farm by taking the next step beyond a yard. I feel complete at my little hobby farm. For others, chickens are just the beginning.

CHICKENS are gateway farm animals. Once you get the hang of hens, you will probably get that itchy curiosity: What's next? The great thing about chickens is you get a fair amount of food for little work and you don't have to kill anybody (well, except for those mealworms). So it follows that the next animal to consider for your urban farm is the duck. Ducks like a little water to play in, which can simply be a shallow wading pool. They lay their eggs on hay, not in a nest box, and their houses are simpler than chicken coops. They don't need to stay as dry as a chicken coop, either, though they need the hay changed regularly. Duck droppings are messier and wetter. Ducks are also noisier. They have pleasanter personalities than chickens, tend to lay more, larger eggs, and their eggs are richer in flavor.

Next on the list of popular hobby farming animals is the goat. Providing milk and wool, goat breeds range in size from 20 to 250 lbs. (9 to 115 kg). Pygmy and dwarf goats have become a popular urban breed. They originate from Africa and the Caribbean and prefer warmer weather, and for their size produce a fair bit of milk. Reservations to raising milk goats include local ordinances against keeping larger livestock, and the issue of selling the kids. In order for a goat to lactate, she must become pregnant. She is bred in the summer through early winter, is pregnant for five months, and produces milk for ten months with two months of rest. The male kids are sold for meat or breed stock, and the females as dairy

Miniature dairy goats have been reported to produce anywhere from $^9/_{10}$ pts. (425 ml), with the average of nearly 6 $^1/_3$ pts. (3 liters) of milk daily. Genetics and management will play an important part in milk production. Unlike many of the standard breeds, Nigerian Dwarfs breed year round, which makes it easier to have a steady supply of milk all year—many of the miniature dairy goats are also year-round breeders.

MINIATURE DAIRY GOAT ASSOCIATION,
WWW.MINIATUREDAIRYGOATS.COM

goats. A ritual of blessing and thanks would be appropriate when selling kids, especially males. Sheep are also raised for milk and wool, and can be kept on a small scale. They can be shorn by hand, though this is rough on your back. Raising sheep for wool leads naturally into spinning, knitting, and felting, a rich hobby farming tradition. Before considering goats or sheep, you should visit a local farm and read up to see if these animals would be a good fit, depending on your needs, lifestyle, and available land. While ruminants need less pasture than one might think, especially the smaller breeds, they still need more than an average suburban yard allows.

Rabbits have been suggested as the next urban hobby farming livestock as they are small and easy to care for. They make lovely pets and offer droppings for compost. However, as food animals, they are raised solely for their meat. One thing

I like about chickens is, as I said, you don't need to slaughter another living being to gain protein. As pets, though, rabbits are a fun choice and loved by children.

Beekeeping is another popular choice for food production. Many cities offer beekeeping classes; and networks of local beekeepers provide skills and equipment, so the suburban beekeeper need not purchase all honey-harvesting equipment herself.

Again we return to the value of the community in urban hobby farms (or any hobby farm for that matter). The size of my yard and local ordinances limit my suburban hobby farm to gardening and chickens. I am not far, however, from several urban farms and community-supported agriculture (CSA) farms, where I can get local honey, milk, and even meat. I can also visit these farms to enjoy spending time with the goats without having to raise and look after them myself. Since I adore goats, this is a very good thing.

SHARING THE LOVE

Activism is another piece of the hobby farming pie, as is support for the endeavors of others. Once you raise chickens and discover how easy and rewarding hen-keeping is, you will want to share your wisdom with others. Online communities, church groups, work friends, and other groups will value your expertise as they too open their yards to a flock of feathered ladies.

S CHOOL GARDENS have become popular, and teach our youth about plants, care for the land, and even economics. I wonder if perhaps the next wave in education might include chickens. Anywhere people gather could house chickens, including schools, community gardens, church gardens, and parks. You need running water, a shed to keep the feed secure, and of course a coop and run area. You need people to care for the hens, something in which many people would enjoy participating.

Such models are already being created. Zenger Farm in Portland, Oregon, is a working urban farm that includes chickens, bees, and turkeys. The Eastside Egg Cooperative, a group of volunteers, cares for the chickens and shares the eggs among themselves. This model of co-operative agriculture will no doubt become more popular as people see the benefits of urban farms and a co-operative economy.

"It's a serious issue—it's no yolk," said Mayor Dave Cieslewicz of Madison, Wisconsin, when his city reversed its poultry ban in 2004. "Chickens are really bringing us together as a community. For too long they've been cooped up."[41]

A major obstacle facing proliferation of the urban farm or hobby farm is simply its public image. People are not used to growing their own food or seeing chickens in an urban yard. The fact that small-scale chicken farming actually reduces rates of salmonella, avian flu, and fecal pathogens is not well known. Concerns about attracting predators and vermin, as well as the fear of vicious birds, may also stop people from raising chickens. But you, the chicken enthusiast, can help change this. You might:

- **Write letters to the editor of your local newspaper supporting small-scale agriculture.**

- **Write a blog about your hen-based hobby farm.**

- **Invite groups to your home to see your yard and your chickens—classrooms, book clubs, and community groups would all value such a visit.**

- **Get involved in local co-operatives, farmers' markets, and the city council to advocate the urban hobby farm.**

- **Form a co-operative in your community to barter eggs, honey, fruit, vegetables, and other food or services.**

Models of food production and consumption are changing in our society today. We want greater responsibility for our food and ourselves. We no longer want to segregate food farms and urban life. We want our lives to reflect our values of nature, community, and health. If we all pooled resources, followed our dreams, and worked together, we could create a world based on peace, co-operation, healthful living, and natural prosperity. The hobby farm will be a part of such a culture. What part do you want to play in this unfolding paradigm?

CHAPTER FOUR

The Chicken
or the Egg?

*It's nearly Ostara, the Celtic holiday of spring
that is more widely known as the Vernal Equinox.
My family and I all ache for real spring. We rejoice
at the sprouting garlic, a scattering of violets, and
another sure sign of spring: more eggs. Our hens, now
nearly a year old, each lay nearly an egg a day. This
increase in production from the past few months comes
from the increasing light as the sun moves northward.
The days are growing longer, night is nearly as long as
day, and we rejoice in this vernal shift each time we
open the egg door to find four brown eggs, one for
each hen. Spring has sprung.*

A SPRING CHICKEN

◆

The symbols of Ostara are tied to the lengthening days and increasing warmth of spring: baby chicks, eggs, bunnies, green grass, and pastel shades of violet, yellow, and pink. These are also the secular symbols of Easter, the Christian holiday of rebirth. Easter comes shortly after Ostara; its date is always the first Sunday following the full moon after the Vernal Equinox. Ostara and Easter are both about rebirth and renewal. Eggs are also celebrated at this time because traditionally Christians would fast for Lent, and enjoy the stockpiled eggs at Easter.

Just as we feel the return of spring, so, too, do the chickens. As Colorado's brown winter grass fills in with green, the hens squawk loudly to be let out of their run. If allowed into the yard, they will peck and scratch for baby dandelion greens, new grass, and spring's emerging bugs. They seem just as

---

To get deeper-hued eggs for Easter or Ostara, put brown eggs in dye for ten minutes. You can play with natural dyes such as beet juice, onion juice, red wine, turmeric boiled in water, cocoa powder, and black tea. For interesting designs wrap your egg in string or onion skins before dropping in the dye, or draw patterns on an egg with wax crayons before dipping it in the color.

It is said that an egg will stand on its end during the
spring (vernal) equinox (about March 21).
This is one of two times in the year when the sun
crosses the equator, and day and night are of
equal length everywhere. Depending on the shape
of the egg, you may be able to stand it on its
end other days of the year as well.

WWW.INCREDIBLEEGG.ORG

excited about the season as we humans, just as restless for
full-on green and warm nights. I've decided not to let them
out, however, in the interest of the pale green garden that will
soon sprout. I know they will decimate the barely unfurled
rhubarb leaves and the tops of my garlic. Instead I throw weeds
and kitchen scraps into the run. They dive for the treats,
tossing the clumps of grass and clover up in the air and fighting
over which of them gets the choicest bites. They would prefer
the yard, but the spacious run gives them joy as well.

A frequent question asked about chickens is whether you
need a rooster to get eggs. The answer is no. I point out that we
human females "lay" an egg each month, and we need a male
around—biologically speaking—only if we want an egg
fertilized (I find human males are good for other reasons
beyond fertilization). Roosters have a bad reputation because
they fight, crow, and harass the ladies. However, chickens were

originally domesticated in Southeast Asia over 8,000 years ago, not for eggs or meat, but for cock-fighting: disputes could be settled and wagers won with roosters.

The cocky boys have spurs on their legs, which can be used to attack adversaries—and from time to time small children. That is not to say that all roosters are nasty in disposition or unfriendly. A friend of mine once had a very dear rooster who liked to be cuddled. Roosters also provide flock management, so they can be useful in a larger flock. But all roosters crow, loudly, at all times of the day (including early morning), so in an urban setting they are best avoided.

THE INCREDIBLE INDUSTRIAL EGG

The egg industry argues that its hens are happy and healthy in their cramped cages. In video footage I've seen of egg factories, the thousands of White Leghorns kept four or more to a metal cage seem healthy enough as they peck at their computer-controlled food and sip at fresh water. They appear clean, and they can even move around a little (albeit not much). The vast metal chicken condominiums do not look as bad as the animal rights coalitions would have us believe. No dead chickens being trampled by their sisters. No piles of discarded roosters. No bleeding hens pecked at by cage mates. True, their beaks look a little odd since they were cut off shortly after hatching, but in general the scene looks clinical rather than inhumane.

O F COURSE, the workers in an egg factory will be careful to remove any dead or mangled birds before any filming takes place, or any students studying the industry visit. The fact is, chickens can live six to a little cage. However, hens that have never seen the light of the sun or a patch of dirt might not know what they are missing. They get regular vet care, food, and water. I do know, though, that my four are so much happier when they can roam my whole yard. They protest about being confined to their 215 sq. ft. (20 m²) run, a run that is vastly larger than a commercial cage. While factory hens are alive and "healthy," I can't imagine they are very happy.

The industrial age turned the simple and natural act of egg-laying into a business. Around the turn of the century, many people kept small flocks of hens for themselves, selling extra eggs to those who did not. Like any industry, eggs slowly moved from small scale to larger as fewer people raised their own hens. In the 1920s and '30s, larger industrial flocks were kept outside, ranging on grass during the day and roosting in coops at night. In such large flocks, disease spread quickly and controlling more aggressive birds was problematic. Since they were outdoors, the chickens were susceptible to predators.

When the hens were moved indoors, their mortality rates fell. Food became "scientifically controlled" and medicines were developed to combat mites and other diseases. In the 1940s egg farmers developed the cage system, which got hens off the floor and eggs away from dirt and feces. Feed became

In 2007 *Mother Earth News* studied eggs "from 14 flocks around the country that range freely on pasture or are housed in movable pens that are rotated frequently to maximize access to fresh pasture and protect the birds from predators." The study found that, compared to conventional, confined eggs, free-range eggs contain:

- One-third less cholesterol
- One-quarter less saturated fat
- Two-thirds more vitamin A
- Two times more omega-3 fatty acids
- Three times more vitamin E
- Seven times more beta carotene.

FROM "MEET REAL FREE-RANGE EGGS," *MOTHER EARTH NEWS* [42]

even more uniform. These advances allowed egg factories to grow to the huge sizes we see today, some containing millions of egg machines—er—hens.

Since cheap food that can be transported and controlled is the point of the food industry, these highly technological advances are touted on egg-industry websites as positive. Animals who produce food on such a large scale are not regarded as animals anymore, so the loss of chicken joy is inconsequential.

Our automated industrial culture has reduced chickens to their product. The eggs are economic units produced by economic units and sold to us (also seen as economic units).

It's no longer about the chicken or the egg, but the money exchangeable for that egg. At Easter time I can buy a dozen eggs for fifty cents. At Whole Foods, a natural-foods market, I can buy a dozen organic shop-brand eggs for three dollars. I can buy local, range-fed organic eggs for five dollars a dozen. Or I can get eggs from my own yard for about a dollar a dozen, the cost of food, and wood shavings.* We celebrate every egg we manage to gather, but in our backyard, the chicken definitely comes first.

In a world where everyone has their own chickens, both the chicken and the egg can come first. Smaller flocks of diverse breeds need fewer antibiotics to stay healthy, and are more easily managed outside, where they can experience the chicken joy of a good dirt bath. We, too, can feel good, feeding them green and growing things, insects, and kitchen scraps. Both the hens and us humans benefit from physical contact, gently stretching out a wing and stroking a warm scaly leg to check for signs of distress. We have a relationship, not just an industry.

Buying Extra Eggs

Many people are realizing that treating animals solely as economic units is unacceptable. Depending on the country, there are now several designations of egg production that are

---

*I calculated the cost of my own eggs by dividing the cost of non-organic food by sixty days and assuming four eggs a day. We don't actually get twenty-eight eggs each week, though—and we get manure for the compost from them as well. So the dollar a dozen is an estimate for comparison purposes.

given to eggs raised under more humane standards. In the winter when our hens' laying reduces, we supplement from the store; I try to buy eggs labeled "Certified Humane," which means:

- **That the producer meets standards of Humane Farm Animal Care and applies these standards from birth through slaughter.**

- **The birds have ample space and shelter, and receive gentle handling to limit stress.**

- **They have ample fresh water and a healthy diet of quality feed, without added antibiotics or hormones.**

- **Cages and crates are forbidden, and animals must be free to do what comes naturally. For example, chickens are able to flap their wings and dust-bathe.** [43]

In the UK, free-range and organic eggs must follow strict rules. A farmer must provide an acre of field for every 400 hens. Many farmers are planting trees for their shade-loving ladies. Electrified fences keep the hens safe from foxes. There is also a large indoor area that includes hay for scratching in and nest boxes for laying; the nest boxes also gather the eggs to keep them cool and clean.

Says the British Free Range Egg Producers' Association, "hens that lay organic eggs are always free-range and the main difference between the two systems is the way in which the hens are kept. Organic hens are fed on a diet based on crops,

which have been grown without the use of artificial fertilizers and pesticides. There are also strict rules about the use of medicine to treat the hens should they get sick.

"Another major difference between free-range and organic is that flock sizes are smaller and the birds have to have more space within the hen house in order to be certified organic. Organic houses are often mobile ... so that they can be moved to fresh pasture between flocks." [44]

By "between flocks" the BFREPA means that after one flock of hens reduces laying (hens lay well for about three years), the house can be moved to fresh pasture before a new flock is moved in, reducing the risk of the spread of disease.

Free-range hens are not necessarily organic, in that they can be fed certain additives such as antibiotics in their food; whereas organic hens in the UK are all free-range and cannot be fed any higher than 5 percent of "non-agricultural ingredients" such as fishmeal. They are given different vaccines that cost more but are "safer." The industry is constantly reassessing rules about flock size, feed purity, and other aspects affecting the health and well-being of egg-layers. So even large-scale egg producers are changing the way hens are treated. Unfortunately, large-scale egg or meat production still lacks totally humane practices. Baby roosters and spent hens, for instance, are not sent to a happy chicken retirement farm. Nor is their slaughter done with much reverence. So while the poultry industry is improving, keeping your own hens is truly the most humane way to go.

THE NUTRITIONAL EGG

◆

In the U.S., 75 billion eggs are produced each year, about the equivalent of 10 percent of the world supply. Thirty million eggs are eaten in the UK each day. Eggs provide quick nutrition, including protein and many essential nutrients. They are high in calcium, phosphorus, potassium, and the vitamins D and B_{12}. Recent studies have found that the high cholesterol content of the yolk does not increase our cholesterol levels. Chicken egg proteins are highly absorbable and easily converted into body tissue.

WHETHER AN EGG is to be fertilized or not, it begins as the yolk, called an oocyte, in the hen's ovary. An unfertilized chicken egg is a single cell. Chickens have one ovary, which expands into the oviduct, a series of pockets and tubes along which a ripe yolk travels as it turns into an egg. The shell consists of calcium carbonate and is deposited in little bits called concretions, which is why eggshells sometimes have little bumps and swirls on them. Once the shell hardens, after about twenty hours, the egg is pushed by peristalsis into the vagina, where it receives the bloom, a coating that keeps bacteria and dust from entering the eggshell's pores. The egg rotates before being laid wide end first.

> Based on the essential amino acids it provides, egg protein is second only to mother's milk as the ideal for human nutrition.
>
> WWW.EGGS.ORG.NZ

The whole cycle takes 24 to 26 hours; when an egg is laid a hen begins the process again after about a half hour of rest, depending on light, available nutrients, and the breed and age of the hen.

Each egg contains about 6.5 grams of protein and 5.8 grams of fat (they are low in saturated fat). They are high in phosphorous, iron, iodine, and the B vitamins. Many women in particular are deficient in iron, iodine, and the B vitamins, so plenty of eggs in the diet can help build health. Higher levels of these nutrients are especially needed during pregnancy and lactation. Eggs are also rich in choline, another important mineral during pregnancy; high choline also reduces the risk of breast cancers. Eggs are high in vitamin D, too, which many people following an indoor, sedentary lifestyle are lacking (since one way we get vitamin D is by spending time in the sun). So, go play with your chickens and then eat some tasty eggs!

Truly free-range, pasture-fed chicken eggs are much higher in most nutrients, such as vitamin D—three to six times as much as typical supermarket eggs—and contain twice as many omega-3 fatty acids. Just as organic vegetables are all-around better for you, eggs produced from chickens living as chickens want to live are just more nutritious. The same is true of most other foods. High-yield agribusiness cows, for instance, produce twenty times the amount of milk needed to feed a

An unfertilized chicken egg is a single cell.

healthy calf, and this increase in volume dilutes vitamin content.[45] Returning to smaller farms and creating urban hobby farms means increased nutrition in all our food.

A recent study, "The Nutritional Properties and Health Benefits of Eggs," conducted by dietitian Dr. Carrie Ruxton and nutritionists Drs. Emma Derbyshire and Sigrid Gibson, found that "eggs can play an important role in weight management and dieting, and could even help prevent age-related macular degeneration—an eye condition that can lead to blindness—thanks to antioxidants found in eggs." [46] According to Paul Pitchford, author of *Healing with Whole Foods*, eggs can even reduce the risk of miscarriage and reduce diarrhea by raising energy in the body.[47]

In Ayurvedic cooking, Sattva means food as medicine for the mind and body. The quality of a person's energy is determined largely by the quality and content of their food, which is affected by its source, modes of processing, and cooking methods. A Sattvic diet is lacto-vegetarian, meaning no meat or eggs are consumed, as "their consumption destroys sentient life." [48] Some diets, however, allow for eggs if they are humanely raised and unfertilized (if you don't have a rooster, obviously).

Fresh, Clean Eggs

Eggs should be stored in the refrigerator, not for food safety reasons as much as freshness. Eggshells are porous, containing thousands of tiny little holes that allow carbon dioxide and moisture to move out and air to move in. This exchange happens faster at room temperature than cooler temperatures, and it happens much faster in washed eggs such as those bought at the supermarket. Hobby or local, small farm eggs that are not washed retain the protective "bloom" and stay fresh longer.*

Hens that are not subjected to electric light in winter will lay less when the sun creeps south. While eggs keep in the refrigerator longer than at room temperature, they will only stay fresh for a couple of months at most. Then the whites get thin and eventually the egg will dry up completely. Also, as an egg dries out, the white's natural bacteria-reducing properties lessen and any bacteria present can grow. This is true of both store-bought and home-flock eggs. To be safe, eat your eggs soon after laying or buying, or freeze them.

Sheelaph Fox of Carrizozo, New Mexico, wrote in to the American homesteader's (hobby farming) magazine *Mother Earth News* to explain how she preserves eggs so that the summer bounty can be saved for the winter months.

"Break two new-laid eggs into a small bowl. Using a clean knife, stir the eggs to roughly mix yolk and white—do not beat. Lightly oil a Pyrex custard cup. Pour in the eggs and freeze. Do as many eggs as you have and want to put up.

---

* Chilling an egg does reduce bacterial growth if salmonella is present, but salmonella in eggs is actually quite rare, especially in backyard eggs when the bloom is not washed off; cooking an egg well is the best way to protect yourself from salmonella and other bacteria.

When frozen solid, tip eggs into a freezer bag, fitting in as many as possible. Zip tight and freeze. You can add frozen eggs until the bag is full. Two eggs seems to be the most useful amount for baking and to eat. They are thawed in the refrigerator, covered, beaten into milk, etc. and used just like fresh eggs, to scramble, make omelets, cakes, and so forth." [49]

If your eggs have any chicken poo on them, you can wash them under running warm water and then use them promptly (at least within a month). To see if an old egg is still edible and safe, place it in a bowl of water. An egg that floats is too old; the air pocket at the base of the egg is large enough to float the egg and indicates the egg has dried too much; the egg will have an unpleasant texture, may be rotten, and has an increased risk of bacteria. You can also hold the egg in front of a light source. This is called candling, and shows how large the air pocket is. A fresh egg will have a little pocket at the bottom, but if the pocket is larger, discard your egg.

The best way to ensure clean eggs is a clean nest box. Change the straw frequently, remove droppings from the box, and gather your eggs daily. Make sure, also, that your egg cartons are clean. I reuse mine but compost or recycle any that have chicken poo, mud, or egg goo in them.

> **"Folk" names for eggs:**
> Cackleberries
> Hen Fruit
> Yellow Eye
> Hen Berries
> Googies

Other eggs besides chickens' include:

- Duck, turkey, and goose, which have a higher fat content and are larger

- Ostrich, each containing the equivalent of two dozen chicken eggs

- Quail, one-fifth of the weight of a chicken's egg

- Black-headed gull, a delicacy in England and Scandinavia

- Iguana eggs, which can be found in open-air markets in South America

- Guinea fowl, emu, and pheasant eggs, found in the markets in parts of Africa.

When our hens first started laying, they gave us tiny eggs. They were so cute! We put them in a carton with large, white, store-bought eggs and took a picture because these little pinkish brown eggs were so precious. I'm not sure if it was me or the hens that were more proud. We tried to determine who might have laid the golden egg—the very first one—but the hens weren't telling. These first few eggs, however, were not only small, but also tended to have imperfections in the shells, as the hens' bodies were not yet used to egg production. One day my daughter opened the nest box door and exclaimed that something disgusting was in the box—upon inspection we determined it was an egg without a shell entirely. To ensure our hens have enough calcium to form complete and relatively unblemished eggshells, we feed them rinsed, crumbled eggshells. Now they lay perfect eggs.

A Perfect Whole

Of course it is for the eating that we go to such lengths to manage, gather, study, and preserve eggs. In addition to being highly nutritious, eggs are versatile. We use them in cakes, desserts, casseroles, and more; for breakfast, lunch, and dinner. All cultures have their ways of preparing eggs: omelets and soufflés in France, frittatas in Italy, stir-fries in China and Thailand, fried "over easy" in the U.S., and poached and boiled in the UK. We divide them to whip up the whites for a light cake or mousse, and use the yolks in puddings and sugar cookies. We paint the whites on bread, use them as leavening and protein and binders, especially in gluten-free baking, and stir them into sauces to thicken them. It is said that a chef's hat, or toque, contains one hundred pleats, each fold representing the many different ways a chef knows to prepare an egg.

Eggs are one of the few forms of animal protein that we can consume in their entirety (smelt, sardines, and soft-shell crabs being others). We do not eat the shell, although in theory we could grind it up and take as a calcium supplement. In my house we either compost the shells or feed them to our hens, so nothing is wasted. But either way, an entire egg is a whole food, the fats in the yolk helping us to assimilate the

What are the psychospiritual effects of consuming eggs? From my observation of people whose major source of animal protein is eggs, I would say that too many eggs encourages a tough and brusque attitude, perhaps overwhelming gentler feelings of kindness, and patience. On the other hand, modest amounts of eggs—just as with meat, fish, and fowl—support aggressiveness, drive, and the ability to run a business to actualize potential energy.

FROM *FOOD AND HEALING,* ANNEMARIE COLBIN [50]

protein in the white. Eggs are so versatile because egg-white proteins contain both hydrophilic (water-loving) and hydrophobic (water-avoiding) amino acids. When you cook an egg, when you add heat to the egg protein, you denature the proteins, folding them up in such a way that the whole bunch of protein becomes hydrophilic. It turns into more solid than liquid because the amino acids are not bonding to water.

The hydrophilic/hydrophobic nature of the proteins in egg whites is also responsible for their ability to whip into a sturdy foam. "When an egg protein is up against an air bubble, part of that protein is exposed to air and part is still in water. The protein uncurls so that its water-loving parts can be immersed in the water—and its water-fearing parts can stick into the air. Once the proteins uncurl, they bond with each other—just as they did when heated—creating a network that can hold the air bubbles in place." [51] Then when you cook whipped egg whites (protein bubbles), the gas inside the bubble expands, the amino acids in the bubble walls denature, and the bubbles do not collapse. This makes for great soufflés, omelets, and gluten-free baking (where the egg proteins provide a structural substitute for the missing gluten protein).

Egg yolks contain lecithin, which has hydrophilic and hydrophobic ends to its molecules. Yolks are used as emulsifiers, something that helps oils and water mix without separating, because lecithin molecules grab on to water on one end and oil on the other, holding the mix stable. This property is why we use yolks in mayonnaise, ice cream, and hollandaise sauce, where we need fats and water to stay evenly mixed.

Eggs are nourishing and versatile, yet fragile and perishable. They are used across cultures, in all sorts of foods and at any time of the day. They contain a sturdy yolk that allows us to blend opposing forces, and a fluffy white that allows us to expand and solidify, all contained in a perfect, natural parcel. It is no wonder, then, that eggs have been regarded as a spiritual metaphor across cultures. An egg is survival, life, potential, and miracle. And extremely tasty, too.

Eggs are nourishing and versatile,
yet fragile and perishable.

THE NOURISHING EGG

◆

We eat a lot of eggs in our house. To us, eggs are a part of home. When he was a child, my husband enjoyed a "real breakfast" made by his father every morning: eggs, bacon, toast. When we got married, he taught me how to make an omelet. Now he cooks eggs almost every morning for our daughter. An egg is a food, but it's also a symbol of nourishment—not only in terms of its nutritional value, but also as an offering of love and care.

EGGS REPRESENT FERTILITY, although today few eggs are fertilized—I wonder what this says about modern culture's attitudes toward our own fertility and creativity? Perhaps nothing. I avoided getting a rooster partly because of the noise, but also because roosters tend to be more violent than their ladies. I didn't want fertile eggs. I cannot help but wonder, though, what it means on an energetic level that the male half of farm animals are generally seen as a problem. Poor boys.

But I digress. Eggs are a sign of rebirth, fertility, and the perfection of roundness. In Zoroastrianism, eggs are painted at the start of the new year, which coincides with the Vernal Equinox, and displayed on a ceremonial table to represent hopes for the new year. In Zoroastrian weddings an egg is circled around a groom's head to ward off evil. The ability of an egg to cleanse the spirit is also part of curanderisma, a system of traditional healing and shamanism in Latin America.

The curandera or curandero passes an egg that has been soaked in holy water over or on the patient's body. Then the egg is cracked open and flushed away, or broken into a glass and "read" for information about the patient's illness.

At the Jewish holy day of Passover, an egg representing sacrifice and new life is included in the ceremonial meal. An egg is also part of Jewish funerals, representing hope through the circle of life.

Our solar system is referred to in Indian spiritual texts as the Egg of Brahma, the Hindu god of creation. Our sun is considered the yolk, with ovoid planetary orbits circling this golden center. Brahma laid this cosmic egg, which will one day be destroyed, then created again, then destroyed, in great cycles of birth and destruction.

> In Ancient Egypt, the symbol of an egg was used to denote an embryo in a woman's womb.
>
> FROM *THE WOMAN'S ENCYCLOPEDIA OF MYTHS & SECTRETS,* BARBARA WALKER [52]

An egg has similarities with the sun. The sun also has three layers, the core (yolk), radiative zone (white), and convection zone (shell). And the story of Brahma's egg has its roots in older myths about Hathor-Astarte's Golden Egg of the Sun. Astarte is one of the oldest forms of the Great Goddess, and is identified with a number of goddesses, including Egyptian Hathor. She is "tirelessly creating and destroying, eliminating the old and generating the new," writes feminist Barbara Walker. Hathor creates the universe just as a hen creates an egg, again and again.

By raising hens we honor the Goddess, fertility, and life. We bring the golden nourishment of the egg into our homes, into our care. We are rewarded with the sun's golden light surrounded by the pale glow of the moon. Interesting that a chicken fed on grass and weeds creates a more golden yolk. The light of the sun, transformed into plant energy through photosynthesis, enters the hen, which then lays the golden egg.

NOURISHING YOUR GOLDEN EGG

As you have seen, the egg is a symbol of light, power, creativity, and fertility. The following egg meditation can be used whenever you feel confused or lost about your direction in life. Just as a hen forms a new egg day after day, you can reshape your dreams anew and redis-cover your footing on your path. Read through the whole meditation once, then remember it or record it, playing it back for yourself.

FIND A PLACE and time where you will not be disturbed. Sit comfortably or lie down and close your eyes. Take several deep breaths, letting the air cleanse the inside of your lungs. Breathe out any old air by pushing on the last bit of your exhale. Now breathe normally, feeling the fresh air enter your body and nourish your blood and cells. Bring your attention to your solar plexus, the spot just below your navel. A large cluster of nerves gathers here, and metaphysically it is your

center of personal power. As you breathe, see your breath gather at this spot. See the solar plexus begin to glow like a yolk-colored sun. Feel the warmth.

Now imagine you are walking down a path in a big, lush garden. Feel your bare feet against the smooth cool stones of the path. You feel comfortable, calm, and alive. Feel your breath flow into your body, bringing in the light of the sun and the breath of the plants. Your solar plexus glows bright and strong. Walk a while on your imagined path, feeling the warm sun and the sweet breeze. Bees buzz in the flowers, turning the sun into golden honey. Birds chirp and call in the trees. All is well.

Then you see up ahead in the grass a little nest. You squat down and peer into the nest, where you discover a golden egg. You look around and see no bird who could have laid it. You sense it is okay to touch it. Brush your fingers over the egg. It is warm. Pick it up and cradle it in your palm.

As you stare at the golden shell, it begins to swirl like oil on water until an image forms. It is a picture of your greatest dreams. Sit with your egg and breathe until the image becomes clear. Let yourself enjoy this picture of your greatest life dream. The image may change. It may include several dreams. Let them come. Let the positive feelings of love and joy flow through you like sunlight as you regard your great dreams. Some of these may be secret, known only to you. Some may even surprise you but feel right. Others may be goals you are working toward now. Allow them all to appear before you.

If no images come, allow for the openness of possibility. You may want to come back to this later. Notice any feelings that arise as you face your dreams. Allow what is to be.

When the egg has swirled back to gold, place it back in the nest and give it thanks. Rise in the garden in your mind, stretch, and breathe. Now come back into your body. Count quietly backward from ten. When you reach one, open your eyes and breathe. With your eyes open, place your hands over your solar plexus. Know that the golden egg of your dreams rests here. As you work and play in life to make your dreams come true, you can return to this center any time to regain encouragement and direction.

Record your meditation in your chicken journal (see pages 57–59). Paint or draw pictures from your dreams. Write down any feelings that arose as you watched your dreams unfold in the golden egg. You may want to return to this garden to explore this further or ask the golden egg for guidance as you walk your path. This egg is your power, your light. You need only breathe the light of the sun into your belly to know its strength.

So now, when you sit yourself down to a plate of eggs, or whip some into a cake, or dye them jeweled tones of pink and blue each spring, you will carry with you a deeper understanding of the power of the unassuming egg. Produced by a bird doing simply what her body does, the egg provides physical and spiritual nourishment. The next time you go to the chicken coop, be sure to thank your hens for their generous gifts!

ON GATHERING EGGS

◆

I decided to raise chickens because I want the best, local, fresh eggs, from my own miniature farm, and because I want my children to know where their food comes from. I want them to stroke a chicken and to help care for these birds. I want my children to know that they are not at the mercy of some unknown industry when it comes to creating a healthful life. And finally, I want to give my kids the singular joy that I had as a child of gathering the eggs.

M AMA!" my four-year-old shouts one morning, "We got FOUR eggs! This one is Tallulah's—it has TWO yolks!" Her face shines with pride and excitement.

And she's right. We crack open the large, brown-shelled egg, and two orange yolks shine brightly in the pan. We crack another egg, whacking it hard on the frying pan's edge to break through the thick shell. This one has only one yolk, but it, too, is dark and solid in substance, surrounded by a very coherent and non-runny albumen.

It gives me great joy to feed my family eggs from our little flock. The eggs taste better, they are higher in vitamins and nutrients, and their carbon footprint is very small. But best of all, my children know where eggs come from. They helped look after the hens that laid their breakfast. They see the difference when we cook with "store-bought eggs" and "chicken eggs" as our daughter calls them. She knows the store-bought eggs were laid by chickens, too —but the reality is so much stronger when we can see the very chickens that laid our eggs from the breakfast table.

It gives me great joy to feed my family eggs from our little flock.

When our hens first started laying eggs, my husband, who loves eggs, felt a little grossed out by the visceral reality of knowing exactly where those eggs came from. It's so much easier, so much "cleaner" to take eggs out of a carton with no thought for the bird that made that egg. This is why as a culture we moved away from backyard hens and toward the automation of industrial egg production. We happily pay someone else to do the dirty work. No droppings to clean, no smell, no mess. No giggling about the cloaca, the single vent from which everything exits the chicken.

But life is messy. I want my children to know how to deal with that mess, both in terms of cleaning the coop and facing their own discomfort about the realities of life. I want my children—and myself—to be okay with dirt, the origins of food, and death, always a counterpart of life. I want to raise compassionate children.

We learn compassion through the care of others. When my child holds a still-warm egg in her hand and looks at the creature that created this egg that she, my daughter, will eat, she knows on a body level the feeling of gratitude. She gets to see the excited such-ness of chickens scrambling for clover or

a peanut-butter sandwich tossed into the run. She begins to understand through direct experience what a chicken really is, the sunlight and dirt and greens and grains that literally go into our hens. She doesn't have to be told to say "thank you" to the hens. Instead she knows the feeling of joy and thanks in her body as she carries the little four-egg basket back to the house. Her grin, her joy, speaks of the sense of gratitude she feels at their gift. Not some heavy thankfulness, but a light and joy-filled exchange of care.

One day my daughter announced that she was going to check for eggs. She grabbed the little egg basket I'd fashioned —a small florist's basket from a cousin's wedding with the end of an egg carton nestled inside, just enough to carry four

---

By learning to respect animals through proper handling, children learn that there are limits and mutual respect in a relationship. By learning to nurture and care for animals, children are being nurtured themselves and learning skills for future relationships. Animals also help children and teens incorporate an understanding of suffering and death into their worldview because they can see that other beings can have pain, illness, and even die, and that they need to be cared for and loved by others.

FROM "THE ROLE OF ANIMALS IN THE EMOTIONAL AND MORAL DEVELOPMENT OF CHILDREN," MOTHER HILDEGARD GEORGE [53]

eggs. A moment later she was back. "There is only two eggs," she announced with some disgust. She plopped the empty egg basket on the work surface. "Why didn't you get them?" I asked. "Because there is only TWO. I have two hands. I can carry two. The egg basket is only for when there are three or four eggs." I argued that she could have gathered those two anyway, since she was out there. She rolled her eyes at my stupidity and went back out to gather the two eggs with her two hands, leaving the unnecessary basket behind. On the way back in, she had some difficulty opening the door with an egg in her hand. The egg slipped out of her grasp and on to the wooden deck. I just shook my head. "Huh—I guess the egg basket is good for two eggs after all," I suggested. She scowled at me and put the single remaining egg in the refrigerator.

My baby loves the chickens, too. One afternoon in very early spring, before my garden had sprouted at all so there was nothing for the hens to destroy, we let the four girls out to roam. My daughter caught Maisy and carried her over to my son and me. A four-year-old carrying a large hen is rather amusing. Maisy looked a bit undignified with her back squashed up against my daughter's chest, her legs poking straight out in front of her, and her wings pinned awkwardly at her sides. My daughter set her down next to us and began to stroke her. Maisy went into the crouch that all hens do, which is actually in preparation to receive a rooster, but works well for stroking, too. My baby batted his hands and squealed, then patted the hen's back gently as only a man still learning fine motor skills can. Maisy looked up at us with her soft orange eyes, wary but trusting. Big sister went off to catch another hen while Maisy, the baby, and I enjoyed each other's company and the early spring warmth.

I told my mom about our son's love of the hens, and she told me that I had been the same. "We would put you in your little chair and set you in front of the chickens. You would sit and watch with rapt attention while we worked in the yard. You loved them." I hadn't realized my hobby farming parents had kept chickens (which, it turns out, were eaten by a fox when I was still a small child). I guess the seeds of compassionate care for the land—and a flock of hens—were planted even earlier than I thought. Now I am planting the same seeds in my children.

When animal researcher Jane Goodall was four years old, she hid in the family chicken coop for hours, buried in hay, to watch a hen lay an egg. She was rewarded as she saw the thrilling sight of an egg emerging from the cloaca. Hens offer a relatively safe opportunity for children to encounter the natural world. Chickens are neither as tame as the family cat nor as wild as a chickadee. The space between offers a doorway of learning where a child can encounter a bird that lives outside but is a part of the family. Goodall learned about the mystery of the hen and the patience required to conduct such scientific research, all from the relative safety of the family chicken coop.

Most of the 8,600 or more species lay eggs shaped about like our familiar "hen fruit," but those of the owls and the Old World bee-eaters are nearly round, and many birds have eggs much longer than they are wide. The auk or murre nests on bare rock ledges of sea cliffs and lays an extremely pointed egg which, if accidentally kicked, will roll a circle instead of over the edge. Plovers and sandpipers also lay pointed eggs. Arranged on the ground, with the points inward, they occupy less space and, although rather large, can be more easily covered by the brooding mother.

FROM "BIRD'S EGGS, THEIR SIZE, SHAPE, AND COLOR," NATURE BULLETIN, FOREST PRESERVE DISTRICT OF COOK COUNTY [54]

I suspect it's only a matter of time before I have to pull my son, six months old as I write this, out of the coop. The door is just the right size for a curious toddler.

Children also learn about responsibility from the family hens. In *Animal, Vegetable, Miracle*, Barbara Kingsolver writes about her youngest daughter's chicken business. Lily carefully chose her egg-layers and decided also to raise some meat birds. "We'll only kill the mean ones," she decided.[55] She wanted to raise enough money to buy a horse.

When I went to see Kingsolver read from her book, I was lucky enough to get to see her family, who had come to celebrate Mother's Day with the author on her book tour.

After Kingsolver's talk someone in the audience asked if Lily had gotten her horse yet. She announced that instead of buying a horse, she had decided to give her profits to charity. She has learned about business, animal care, and discovered the joy of compassionate giving.

Children learn through doing and by watching what we do. With carefully tended hens in the backyard, children learn, among other things:

- **Economics** - **Pet care** - **Politics** - **Ecology**
- **Gardening** - **Landscape design** - **Carpentry**
- **Self-sufficiency** - **Sharing**

> Shortly after we began raising chickens … our town passed an ordinance banning all farm animals (including chickens) from city limits. My youngest daughter, aged ten at the time, took the initiative to write a speech for presentation to the Town Council. At the town meeting, she was the first person to speak on the ordinance. She calmly presented what she had been learning from raising chickens. The Town Council was impressed with her argument, and a local television news reporter came out to our house to interview our daughter. The council ended up reversing its decision, and my daughter played a significant part in that decision.
>
> NUTUBA, A BLOGGER ON HUBPAGES.COM [56]

For a collection of chicken and egg related educational resources, see *www.kiddyhouse.com/Farm/Chicken/*. The site includes chicken facts for kids, and a list of printables, songs, crafts, and more.

Mostly they learn about a world where small is beautiful, where animals have souls or at least intrinsic value, where we are responsible for more than ourselves, and where our choices and actions make a difference.

The beauty of keeping chickens and growing an organic garden with children is that I don't have to do any formal instructing. They just learn by doing. They learn through ecological validity—the learning tool is embedded in their lives, not just a film or book about something they never encounter. Of course I can take a subject such as chickens and teach math or science (we need to measure the feed; how many eggs do we have?; look at the patterns on her feathers) or writing (c-h-i-c-k-e-n) that relates to something she cares about, but the deeper learning, the kind most important for young children, happens through daily interaction with something fun and fascinating.

Children are our little eggs, carrying inside radiant shells our hopes for a full and healthy future. If you don't have children of your own, consider sharing your hen-keeping with other children in your life. You might:

• **Help a school keep hens, or invite a class to visit yours.**

• **Give a presentation at a library about your hens and their eggs. Discuss how important it is to be kind to animals, and how healthy free-range eggs are.**

• **Invite neighborhood children or nieces and nephews to gather eggs and feed the hens. Give them a chance to stroke the chickens and hold a warm egg.**

Children exposed to compassionate caring for animals and food sources will grow up to be responsible adults who care for the earth, each other, and all other life forms. This may be the greatest gift you could give the child.

> To Touch and Feel is to Experience. Many people live out their entire lives without ever really Touching or being Touched by anything. These people live within a world of mind and imagination that may move them sometimes to joy, tears, happiness, or sorrow. But these people never really Touch. They do not live and become one with life.
>
> FROM *SEVEN ARROWS*, HYEMEYOHSTS STORM [57]

Chicken-Related Books for Children

You can learn a lot through doing, but also learn much from reading good children's books. The books on the opposite page are all engaging books starring chickens.[58]

- *Tillie Lays an Egg* by Terry Golson, photos by Ben Fink
- *The Chicken of the Family* by Mary Amato, illustrated by Delphine Durand
- *Chicken Cheeks* by Michael Ian Black, illustrated by Kevin Hawkes
- *Chicken Butt* by Erica S. Perl
- *How the Ladies Stopped the Wind* by Bruce McMillan, illustrated by Gunnella
- *Chicky Chicky Chook Chook* by Cathy MacLennan
- *Minerva Louise* by Janet Morgan Stoeke (there is a whole series of Minerva Louise books)
- *Daisy Comes Home* by Jan Brett
- *The Problem With Chickens* by Bruce McMillan, illustrated by Gunnella
- *Why Did the Chicken Cross the Road?* Many illustrator-authors, Dial Books for Young Readers
- *The Painter Who Loved Chickens* by Olivier Dunrea
- *Big Chickens, Big Chickens Fly the Coop,* and *Big Chickens Go to Town* by Leslie Helakoski, illustrated by Henry Cole
- *Hattie and the Fox* by Mem Fox
- *Rosie's Walk* by Pat Hutchins
- *My Life as a Chicken* by Ellen Kelley
- And finally, the Maisy books, such as *Maisy's Morning on the Farm,* by Lucy Cousins. Maisy is a mouse, but her best friend Tallulah is a chicken, and it is after these two lovely characters that we named two of our hens.

CHAPTER FIVE

THE MIND OF THE CHICKEN IS UNGRASPABLE

The mind of the past is ungraspable;
the mind of the future is ungraspable;
the mind of the present is ungraspable.

"THE DIAMOND SUTRA" [59]

THE UNGRASPABLE NOW

My six-month-old loves wind chimes, finials, and chickens. When he's fussy and bored, I'll carry him out to the coop to watch our four birds. He stares with rapt attention, a droplet of drool dangling from his bottom lip, his arms and legs twitching in excitement. Just as he soaks in the world, I soak in his chubby, sweet self. His downy hair, round Buddha cheeks, and bright smile could melt the hardest soul. I can scarcely believe how fast he is growing up; I've blinked and we're here.

I REALIZE THIS BABY I hold as he croons back at the hens will be gone in a few years, a few months, a few days—grown into a little boy and then a man. This exact baby is only this exact baby right now. The same is true of anything in this moment. It will never repeat itself. Suddenly the slipperiness of time asserts itself. I understand on a deep level the ungraspable nature of this moment, my thoughts, even the seemingly solid chunky baby in my arms. I feel a swerve of vertigo. Knowing that this moment will be gone in an instant, I sit fully in the instant as it unfolds and is gone. The moment is like the shifting green light on the iridescent black feathers of my Black Austrolorpe, or the clouds that shift and dance overhead.

When I fully inhabit the present moment as it unfolds and passes, I am filled with the miracle of the now. My heart explodes with the cherished treasure of this instant. Not just of the beloved baby in my arms, or the joy of our hobby farm, or the sweetness of spring air, but the very particles of this instant become sacred to me. I feel I am bathing in God.

Then, just as quickly, I am back in my thoughts, enmeshed in space-time. My ego and my mind take over again, driving me through each day. My thoughts turn to my to-do list (sort baby clothes, fill out those forms, call a friend). I am still filled with love for my baby, but the vertigo of the ungraspable-ness of each moment, of everything, passes.

Underlying my thoughts, though, hums the field of all possibilities. The energy I tapped into as I became aware of the slipperiness of time is a sense I can enter into at any moment by focusing on that hum. Doing so gives me perspective. I feel, simultaneously at the same moment, both the small-ness of this dot that is my

> [The] universe exists in some vast "here" where here represents all points of space and time at a single instant.
>
> FROM *THE FIELD*, LYNN MCTAGGART [60]

home, my life, my neighborhood, and the deep consequential weight of everything. Each subatomic particle has a place and a value. Yet all of it changes, lets go, moves onward, inward, in a great dance. The only dance there is.

All of the spiritual traditions of the world are ultimately aimed at seeking unity with the universe, or God, or the Goddess. Each path has its own tools like meditation or prayer, and each has its dogma, or ways of looking at the world.

Ultimately, though, the goal is the same. Our challenge as humans is to move toward unity using these tools and yet releasing them at the same time so that we do not get hung up on them. We don't want the tools to become the path. That is why it is said one must kill the Buddha: the teachings in and of themselves are not the truth, only the teachings integrated in yourself. Yet to get to where we're going, we need the lighthouse of teachings and tools.

Spiritual teacher Ram Dass says about different spiritual systems, "My general way of dealing with this is to ignore most of it. I mean I don't learn all of these systems because I'm not terribly interested. Because whatever it is that I see in 'form,' I've got to go beyond it, anyway, so why bother chronicling it?" [61] For, he says, "Here is the predicament that one faces about this [spiritual] work. The goal of these efforts is a non-dualistic state … To get to that place you use methods that are in dualism. Right? You use dualism to talk about it. You use dualism to go beyond dualism." [62]

Your life is your practice because it doesn't matter if the dualism you use (the tools, the paradigm, the beginning state of consciousness) to get to unity or non-dualism is holding a baby or meditating. It is how you approach the path that matters. Whether your spiritual practice is prayer in a church or meditation at an ashram or gathering hens' eggs, what matters is showing up with compassion for yourself and others. What matters is fully showing up.

> Well, I was six years old. I was in the kitchen and I was
> watching my little sister in her high-chair drink milk.
> I suddenly saw, that it was sort of like God pouring God
> into God, if you know what I mean.
>
> RAM DASS PARAPHRASING J.D. SALINGER'S "TEDDY" [63]

By compassion I mean not simply caring, but love. God's love, if you will, that inhabits us all. When I sink into that love, all is practice. Everything is then "spiritual" from that place.

My life is my practice because it isn't easy to stay in the hum of higher consciousness when I have a list of things to do. When I have to clean out the chicken run or change a diaper or deal with the sassiness of my four-year-old, I rarely operate from the iridescent light of All Love. I aspire to, but so frequently I fail. Which, I realize, is part of the practice, too. I pick myself up, brush myself off, and start all over again.

This is the real point of any spiritual work. It is the point of hobby farming and raising chickens. It is why we do anything: to return to love, and to seek the Infinite in all we do. Living life from this place makes a life of meaning and intrinsic value. All becomes sacred. Our breath, each step we take: all is right livelihood. We return to center and right living.

It is why we do anything: to return to love,
and to seek the Infinite in all we do.

A COMPASSIONATE LIFE

◆

When I know God is everything, every moment, each breath, each parcel of the universe—even if I don't feel this unity in every moment—I feel a sense of responsibility to the sacred moment. I feel the need to care for and act compassionately toward each moment and every thing. I feel this not in a way that will drain me, but in a way that will feed me. Filled with the infinite love of each particle of being, I am able to serve life in a way that serves myself. Both literally and spiritually, when I feed the hens, I feed myself. When I steward the garden, I steward the whole earth and myself. Ironically, from this perspective, when I serve myself I do so not in the narcissism of the ego, but in the selflessness of unity with Spirit.

A T THE BEGINNING of the book, I posed the question of what it means to take responsibility for our lives, the earth, and ourselves. Here lies the answer: responsibility is seeking communion with the sacred now and acting compassionately from that center. That will look different to each person. For me a responsible life includes lovingly tended chickens, children, a garden, a marriage built on respect, and living as "green" as I can. The challenge for me, then, as for anyone, is not to get too attached to the actions that grow from responsible, compassionate living, but to remain centered in

All is miracle. All is spiritual path.

the consciousness that underlies and germinates those actions. I am responsible when I choose repeatedly to return to that center as best I can. I

> The earth keeps some vibration going
> There in your heart, and that is you.
>
> FROM *SPOON RIVER ANTHOLOGY*,
> EDGAR LEE MASTERS [64]

know I'm too attached to the actions when I start beating myself up about, say, not using cloth diapers all the time, or using my dryer instead of hanging the clothes out, or "only" keeping chickens (not ducks or goats), or buying eggs from the stores sometimes. These things make a difference, but no one can be perfect all the time. When we get attached to rules for being perfect, we lose sight of the compassion behind these measures. That needs to include compassion for myself. I return to the path by tuning in to the vastness of the compassionate universe and know all is well. Which is not to say we can just live any which way and it will all turn out fine. Maybe we can, and maybe it will, but this is not living a life of compassion.

Remember Thich Nhat Hanh's dishwashing meditation: "The dishes themselves and the fact that I am here washing them are miracles!" I do not seek spiritual enlightenment from the dishes themselves. How I approach them, though, can bring me to deeper, compassion-centered relationship with the miracle of the universe. The same is true of anything: yoga, prayer, cleaning out the chicken coop. All is miracle. All is spiritual path.

A compassionate life can look like almost anything as long as we return to the miracle of each moment. This centers us in what is right and true, and all things flow from that point. I return to Ram Dass: "You realize that the only thing you have to do for other human beings is to keep yourself really straight, and then do whatever it is you do." [65] So you might ride motorcycles or raise chickens or do yoga or home-school your children or … just do whatever it is that you do from your heart, from compassion, from right livelihood. That life will bring you home.

The rub is that we still have to deal with anger and messy coops and cranky chickens and whatever else lies across the path. Life is messy. I find I can better deal with the messiness of life, though, when I hold in my heart the sacredness of all, from a chick to a rooster and the sun to which he crows.

When I feel overwhelmed by all I have to do, or feel burdened by my wants tugging away at my heart and slowing me down—I want to sit down and read a book, not take care of the children; I want to move to another city but we're here for my husband's amazing job; whatever—I try to hold in my heart the big picture. I remind myself that the children will be grown one day, and I will have lots of time to read, wondering if they're going to call their old mother.

I remind myself of all the great things about the city I live in, which isn't the home of my heart but is my home. I am meant to be here now, doing these things that I chose. Then

> It's just that when you really start to take the
> warrior's journey—which is to say, when you start
> to want to live your life fully instead of opting for
> death, when you begin to feel this passion for life
> and for growth, when discovery and exploration
> and curiosity become your path—then basically, if
> you follow your heart, you're going to find that it's
> often extremely inconvenient.
>
> FROM *THE WISDOM OF NO ESCAPE*, PEMA CHÖDRÖN [66]

I take a deep breath and I get up and just do something. I feed
the hens or weed the garden or make dinner, and in the doing,
I return to the moment.

Most days I'm just tired. I want to sit down and do nothing
or maybe burst into tears. But I hold the big picture in mind
—I chose to have children, stay home with them, and create
a big yard with chickens because these choices are deeply central to who I am as a person living a compassionate—and
passionate—life. Then I pull on my boots and go out to lock
up the hens, when really I'd rather go to bed; the moon is
bright and crisp, and the night smells of wood smoke, and I
hear the hens rustling slightly in the dark of the coop, and
I feel my restlessness settle. The sacredness of all rises spontaneously in my heart and I remember to breathe again.

CENTERING MEDITATION

◆

Have you ever noticed that life keeps raising the stakes? As soon as you congratulate yourself for a job well done, the next little task shows up at the doorstep. Often this comes in the form of relationship challenges—a difficult four-year-old, a chicken on the loose, a cranky husband—and remember, all is relationship. When this happens to me, I can so often feel anger, resentment, and indignation. "I thought I'd mastered this," I say, throwing up my hands. In those moments I find it valuable to consciously recenter myself. Here is a practice I use to return to the miracle of the moment.

Take a deep breath. And another. Close your eyes and breathe, feeling the air enter your lungs. Notice the constriction in your body. I often carry anger in my chest and belly. Where does it sit for you? Notice. Breathe. As you notice, you will naturally release: your jaw, your chest, wherever.

As you release, a new wave of emotion will probably arise. This might be shame, sadness, or something else. Notice it. Hold it like a dry leaf in your hands. Let yourself sink deeper. Let your breath guide you. Be curious about that sensation.

Keep going deeper. Deep breaths will spontaneously arise as you settle into quieter parts of yourself. Images, memories, and sensations will come forth. Sit with them and let them be without clinging to them. If you find yourself wrapped up in a thought or memory, just notice that and come back to your breath. Return to the sensation in your body. Stay with what is there. The purpose of meditation is not to get rid of all the discomfort, but to simply notice what is. Do that by breathing and returning again and again to yourself. Be curious and compassionate with yourself.

Finding the Sacred Now

It can be helpful to have an image or feeling, a sort of touch point, from which you can find the sacred miracle of all that is. For me that touch point came when looking at my baby. From the present aliveness of my baby, I was able to see the ungraspable nature of the universe, the mind, and reality as we know it. When I need perspective, once I calm down using my breath, I re-enter conscious relationship with the sacred by focusing on the image of my baby. I have had other touch points before, such as images encountered in meditation. I hold that image and then I get a feeling in my body, a sort of shift point, from where my consciousness changes.

When I struggled with the idea of raising chickens, I found a still, centered place in myself where I could breathe and be quiet. There were so many different factors chattering in my head: I was about to have a baby, this was a substitute for my bigger dream life that I felt was currently unattainable, the neighbors might complain, etc. In the stillness of the moment, I let all that go. In the calm of that space it felt right and doable to raise chickens. Whenever I started to balk at the details over the next few months (and even after I got the birds), I retuned to this, still knowing that all was well. What image or experience has brought you into the sacred now? Can you recall a time, a person, a feeling, a quote, something that brought you up against the infinite? This might be something like:

- **A sense you got while praying or meditating.**
- **A late-night conversation with a loved one.**
- **An image of something larger than yourself:**
  sunrise, the ocean, the birth of a child.
- **A dream you once had.**
- **A time when an animal appeared to you suddenly,**
  either in nature or your imagination.
- **The image of your hens scratching, seeing**
  the world through their eyes, or the smooth feel
  of their feathered backs.

That touch point can be anything. Even washing the dishes! You will feel that shift in your belly, that vertigo, as you enter into the bigger picture. Your ego lets go just a bit. You touch God. You take a deep breath and there you are.

Take a moment to write down or draw your touchstone. Remember, the touchstone is not the important bit—kill the Buddha—the important thing is the energy, the feeling, the relationship with the Infinite. New layers may come up as you draw or write. You gain insight into your relationship with yourself and the world as you explore your experiences. The writing practice helps you to reflect.

THE RIVER OF TIME

The mind is ungraspable. Time is an illusion, or at least a tool allowing us to interact with the single point of the quantum universe. Matter is energy, also something of an illusion. Sit in your center and contemplate these ideas. When they all sink in, even a little bit, we realize the malleability of the world. We realize "the future" is not such a fixed thing, toward which we swim in the river of fate. Instead of the fish in the river of time, we are the water. We help shape the banks, not simply bounce against them.

As I touched on earlier, I believe strongly in the power of visualization and intention to manifest one's own reality. I tap into this power through collage, keeping a journal, and drawing. And I write out my intentions, paste photos of my dreams, and draw pictures of my desires. It helps me to organize my thoughts and direct my intentions. My heart knows what I want. My mind knows where we're headed. My body follows suit. The energy of my dreams vibrates in my cells, and by the time I get to that place in my life where I can make something reality, I'm ready to turn my dreams into actions.

I dreamed of chickens for a long time. I pictured my children playing with them. I read about them. I looked at pictures of coops. When the free wood to build a coop became available, I jumped at the possibility. Had I not been dreaming of hens for years, I probably would not have taken my friend's scrap wood. What would I have done with it? Not build a chicken coop. How could I make a coop? Not me. But I did not have these negative thoughts because the seed idea of chickens had grown to a big old weed in my mind and I was fully ready to pluck it.

The mind is ungraspable, but the patterns it creates, that we create with the power of the mind, lay down stepping stones for us to follow. Then we choose to follow the path, and … we're there. Everything important in my life has been this way. I set out to do it, dream it, and make it happen. It's the dialectic of reality: all is an ungraspable flow unfolding moment to moment, yet we can participate in and shape that flow by riding the waves of the ungraspable now and by having the intention of where to steer the craft. We have to let go and yet guide our path at the same time. You set up the chicken coop and cover the nest box with straw, then you step back and trust that eggs will come in their own chickenish time.

The mind is ungraspable, but the patterns it creates, that we create with the power of the mind, lay down stepping stones.

THE WAY OF THE HEN

◆

We hen-keepers hold as one of our centers or touch points the care of
chickens. In doing so we drop a stone into the pond of life that sends
out ripples of care for the earth and all her beings. We shape the
riverbank of life with our convictions and our dreams through
the simple act of raising chickens. Daily we face the reality of inter-
dependence; we understand that all is interconnected, from the
microbes in the soil to the sun in the sky and all life in between.
All is Spirit, even the simple hen.

WHEN YOU HOLD a hen in your lap or feel her warm egg in your palm, you know, on some deep level, the power and importance of every particle of creation. This egg is the egg of a beautiful world. It is the cosmic ovum of existence. Though most days we just gather the eggs and move on with the daily machinations of life, every once in a while we hold a fresh egg in our hands and we feel the pulse of the miracle of life. You could maybe call this The Way of the Hen.

The Way of the Hen is about small-scale hen-keeping in the name of greater personal responsibility for the earth, our food, and our communities. It is a path of beauty that embraces the down and dirty. The Way of the Hen honors worms and soil as sacred, and sees the backyard as a microcosm for the entire universe. We honor compassion, sustainability, and wise use of resources. Many of us, too, hold a certain hope,

137

however utopian, that everyone might one day know their food. That one day we will all honor the wisdom and intrinsic value of all life in all we do. And that the lowly hen might take her rightful place atop the roost of everyday life.

The Way of the Hen is a silly name for a deeply important practice, the raising of hens on a small scale, where the chicken is known and cared for. This practice is both metaphor and tangible act leading us as a species to live more peaceably and humanely on the planet. Raising chickens makes a difference: in your heart and spirit, in the lives of others around you, for the chickens, and for the land.

Thank you for walking with me on the Way. I wish you joy and enlightenment on your journey. When the going gets tough, return to your center. Go and sit under the apple tree and stroke a hen. Let her crooning remind you of all that is real and sacred. Remember to "express your true nature in the simplest, most adequate way and to appreciate it in the smallest existence"[67] and all will be well.

May the eggs be fresh, the hens happy, the grass green, and may all you do be blessed. Namaste.

SOURCES & ENDNOTES

1 Shunryu Suzuki. *Zen Mind, Beginner's Mind: Informal Talks on Zen Meditation Practice*. New York: Weatherhill, 1980. 48.

2 Susan Orlean. "The It Bird: The return of the back-yard chicken." *The New Yorker*. September 28, 2009. 29.

3 Suzuki, 1980. 33.

4 Karen Maezen Miller. *Momma Zen*. Boston: Trumpeter, 2007. 6.

5 Lynn Brunelle. *Yoga for Chickens*. San Francisco: Chronicle Books, 2004. 9.

6 Brunelle. 2004. 20.

7 E.B. White. "The Hen (An Appreciation)." 1944. Quoted in *On Writing Well: The Classic Guide to Writing Nonfiction*. William Knowlton Zinsser. New York: Harper Collins, 2006. 26.

8 Clare W. Graves. Quoted in "About Spiral Dynamics Integral." http://tinyurl.com/372yexd.

9 Yabukoji. *The Zen Master Hakuin: Selected Writings*. Trans. Philip B. Yampolsky. New York and London: Columbia University Press, 1971. 164. Find on the website via the reference: http://www.io.com/~snewton/zen/onehand.html.

10 Suzuki. 1980. 106.

11 Brunelle. 2004. 61.

12 "Using Chicken Manure as Garden Fertilizer." http://poultryone.com.

13 Matthew Fox. *A Spirituality Named Compassion: And the Healing of the Global Village, Humpty Dumpty and Us*. San Francisco: Harper & Row, 1979.154.

14 Herman E. Daly. "Sustainable Economic Development: Definitions, Principles, Policies." *The Essential Agrarian Reader: The Future of Culture, Community, and the Land*. Norman Wirzba, ed. Washington, DC: Shoemaker & Hoard, 2004. 64.

15 Carol Ann Sayle. "Why Backyard Chickens are a Trend." *The Atlantic*. May 18, 2009. http://tinyurl.com/362gwzr.

16 "Chicken Diapers." MyPetChicken.com. Accessed February 6, 2010.

17 Charlotte Joko Beck. *Everyday Zen: Love and Work*. New York: Harper SanFrancisco, 1989. 89.

18 Joko Beck. 1989. 77.

19 Suzuki. 1980. 23.

20 Pam Percy. *The Complete Chicken: An Entertaining History of Chickens*. Stillwater, MN: Voyageur Press Inc., 2002. 10–11.

21 Peter Lennox. "Pecking Order." *Times Higher Education*. February 4, 2010. www.timeshighereducation.com.uk.

22 Froma Walsh. "Human-Animal Bonds I: The Relational Significance of Companion Animals." *Family Process*; December 2009, Vol. 48 Issue 4, 466.

23 Walsh. 2009.

24 Vince Devlin. "Feathered Friends: Chickens trained by Polson woman to provide therapy." *The Missoulian*. June 19, 2009. http://missoulian.com.

25 "Handicapped Chicken Contest." April 11, 2009 on backyardchickens.com.

26 Tarthang Tulku. *Openness Mind*. Berkley, CA: Dharma Publishing, 1978. 121.

27 Thich Nhat Hanh. *Peace Is Every Step: The Path of Mindfulness in Everyday Life*. New York: Bantam, 1992. 26.

28 Thich Nhat Hanh, 1992. 69.

29 Cindy Anderson. Post on public chicken message board. With permission.

30 John Welwood. *Love and Awakening: Discovering the Sacred Path of Intimate Relationship*. New York: Harper Perennial, 2006. xiii.

31 Soiku Sigematsu, trans. *Zen Forest*. Quoted in *Chop Wood Carry Water: A Guide to Finding Spiritual Fulfillment in Everyday Life*. Rick Fields et al. Los Angeles: Jeremy P. Tarcher, 1984. xi.

32 Rebecca Kneale Gould. *At Home in Nature: Modern Homesteading and Spiritual Practice in America*. Berkeley and Los Angeles: University of California Press, 2005. xviii.

33 Gould. 2005. 23.

34 Gould. 2005. 33.

35 Gould. 2005. 2.

36 "Dig, Dig, Dig for Victory." http://tinyurl.com/dd7dln.

37 "Yes, we can." October 1, 2009. www.henwaller.com.

38 "Farmers' Markets." Local Harvest. http://tinyurl.com/27k7jwh.

39 Gould. 2005. xxi.

40 Joanna Macy. "The Greening of the Self." *Ordinary Magic: Everyday Life as Spiritual Path*. Ed. John Welwood. Boston: Shambhala, 1992. 270.

41 Quoted in "U.S. City Dwellers Flock to Raising Chickens" by Ben Block. October 6, 2008. www.worldwatch.org/node/5900.

42 Cheryl Long and Tabitha Alterman. "Meet Real Free-Range Eggs." *Mother Earth News*. October/November 2007. http://tinyurl.com/2ax2ury.

43 "What is Certified Humane Raised and Handled?" *Humane Farm Animal Care*. www.certifiedhumane.org. Accessed 13 March 2010.

44 www.theranger.co.uk/consumers/print.htm.

45 Cheryl Long and Lynn Keiley. "Is Agribusiness Making Food Less Nutritious?"

Mother Earth News. June/July 2004. http://tinyurl.com/32w2sw5.

46 "New research finds eggs are a superfood." British Lion Eggs.
www.nutritionandeggs.co.uk.

47 Paul Pitchford. *Healing with Whole Foods: Oriental Traditions and Modern Nutrition*.
Berkeley, CA: North Atlantic Books, 1993. 112.

48 Pitchford. 1993. 602.

49 Sheelaph Fox. "How to Freeze Eggs for Winter Use." *Mother Earth News*.
August/September 2001. http://tinyurl.com/2cjozq3.

50 Annemarie Colbin. *Food and Healing*. New York: Ballantine, 1996. 167.

51 "Science of Eggs." *Science of Cooking*. http://tinyurl.com/262gynm.

52 Barbara J. Walker. "Astarte." *The Women's Encyclopedia of Myths & Secrets*. New
York: Harper San Francisco, 1983. 69–70.

53 Hildegard George. (1999). "The role of animals in the emotional and moral
development of children." In F.R. Ascione & P. Arkow (eds.), *Child abuse, domestic
violence, and animal abuse: Linking the circles of compassion for prevention and
intervention* (383). Indiana: Purdue University Press.

54 Roland F. Eisenbeis and George W. Dunne. "Birds' Eggs, Their Size, Shape, and
Color," *Nature Bulletin No. 455-A*, Forest Preserve District of Cook County. April
29, 1972. http://tinyurl.com/39dlvah.

55 Barbara Kingsolver. *Animal, Vegetable, Miracle: A Year of Food Life*. New York:
Harper Collins, 2007. 95.

56 Nutuba. "A Case for Raising Chickens." http://tinyurl.com/37dq5pp.

57 Hyemeyohsts Storm. From *Seven Arrows*. Quoted in *The Earth Speaks*. Eds.
Steve Van Matre and Bill Weiler. Greenville, WV: The Institute for Earth
Education, 1983. 29.

58 Thanks to Terry Golson, author of *Tillie Lays an Egg*, for compiling most of this
list. See www.chickenkeeping.com/fun.htm.

59 Quoted in Joko Beck. 1989. 82.

60 Lynn McTaggart. *The Field: The Quest for the Secret Force of the Universe*. New
York: Harper Collins, 2002. 164.

61 Ram Dass. *The Only Dance There Is*. New York: Anchor Books, 1974. 33.

62 Dass. 1974. 31.

63 Dass. 1974. 4.

64 Edgar Lee Masters. *Spoon River Anthology*. New York: MacMillan, 1967. 65.

65 Dass. 1974. 6.

66 Pema Chödrön. *The Wisdom of No Escape: And the Path of Loving-Kindness*. Boston:
Shambhala, 1991. 91.

67 See note 42.

INDEX

FURTHER READING

Zen, Buddhism, & Spirituality

Charlotte Joko Beck. *Everyday Zen: Love and Work*. New York: Harper-SanFrancisco, 1989.

Clea Danaan. *Voices of the Earth: The Path of Green Spirituality*. Woodbury, MN: Llewellyn Worldwide, 2009.

Ram Dass. *The Only Dance There Is*. New York: Anchor Books, 1974.

Matthew Fox. *A Spirituality Named Compassion: And the Healing of the Global Village, Humpty Dumpty and Us*. San Francisco: Harper & Row, 1979.

Thich Nhat Hanh. *Peace is Every Step: The Path of Mindfulness in Everyday Life*. New York: Bantam, 1991.

Karen Maezen Miller. *Momma Zen*. Boston: Trumpeter, 2007.

Agriculture, Smallholding, & Gardening

Carleen Madigan (ed.). *The Backyard Homestead*. North Adams, MA: Storey Publishing, 2009.

Clea Danaan. *Sacred Land: Intuitive Gardening for Personal, Political & Environmental Change*. Woodbury, MN: Llewellyn Worldwide, 2007.

Rebecca Kneale Gould. *At Home in Nature: Modern Homesteading and Spiritual Practice in America*. Berkeley and Los Angeles: University of California Press, 2005.

Toby Hemenway. *Gaia's Garden: A Guide to Home-Scale Permaculture*. White River Junction, VT: Chelsea Green, 2000.

Barbara Kingsolver. *Animal, Vegetable, Miracle: A Year of Food Life*. New York: Harper Collins, 2007.

Hen-Keeping

Martin Gurdon. *Hen and the Art of Chicken Maintenance: Reflections on Raising Chickens*. Guilford, CT: Lyons Press, 2005.

Barbara Kilarski. *Keep Chickens! Tending Small Flocks in Cities, Suburbs, and Other Small Spaces*. North Adams, MA: Storey Publishing, LLC. 2003.

Jay Rossier. *Living with Chickens: Everything You Need to Know to Raise Your Own Backyard Flock*. Guilford, CT: Lyons Press, 2004.